Effective Leadership
A Cure for the NHS?

DENISE CHAFFER

Foreword by
BARONESS EMERTON
Life Peer
President, Florence Nightingale Foundation
Dame British Empire, Dame Grand Cross Order
of St John of Jerusalem

CRC Press
Taylor & Francis Group
Boca Raton   London   New York

CRC Press is an imprint of the
Taylor & Francis Group, an **informa** business

CRC Press
Taylor & Francis Group
6000 Broken Sound Parkway NW, Suite 300
Boca Raton, FL 33487-2742

© 2016 by Denise Chaffer
CRC Press is an imprint of Taylor & Francis Group, an Informa business

No claim to original U.S. Government works

Printed on acid-free paper
Version Date: 20160126
Printed and bound by CPI Group (UK) Ltd, Croydon, CR0 4YY

International Standard Book Number-13: 978-1-78523-159-9 (Paperback)

Visit the Taylor & Francis Web site at
http://www.taylorandfrancis.com

and the CRC Press Web site at
http://www.crcpress.com

Contents

Looks at some of the current thinking and theory on successful
leadership, and includes thinking on what makes organisations
succeed or fail, and the features of good and bad leaders

Co-authored with Dr Suzette Woodward

Looks in more detail at some of the problems specific to nursing
and medicine leadership and of the context and environment in
which they operate

Includes the unique views of a number of highly successful senior
healthcare leaders, who have many years of senior level experience
in relation to healthcare provision

  Former Chairman, Heart of England NHS Foundation Trust and Member of the
  House of Lords

6   **Confirming the diagnosis: what problems need to be addressed?**
Pulls together the evidence from the literature and the themes arising from the lived experience of these key leaders to complete the diagnosis

This chapter makes a number of recommendations based on evidence from some of the theory and the experiences of the key healthcare leaders to help build a more effective leadership of health organisations. It also proposes a framework for selection and monitoring of the leadership team, the aim being to provide a consistent approach, and one that not only supports effective recruitment of the best candidates but also provides early warning monitoring systems upon which to act

Foreword

The delivery of high-quality care is always an important facet of patient care. This book is an essential read for everyone engaged in the leadership of delivery of patient care from the 'bed to the Board'. In recent enquiries, much criticism has been levied both at whole organisations or small units within them. Subsequent enquiries have raised a range of recommendations to address these issues.

Denise Chaffer, the author of this book, has not only addressed personally the subject of leadership whilst undertaking a Florence Nightingale Leadership Scholarship but has further explored the 'Why and the How' in the pursuit of excellence experienced by a range of leaders in healthcare who have contributed from their wide and different experiences to this book. The challenges that have been encountered and the pathways taken by these individuals make a fascinating read and present a challenge in one way or another to all healthcare professionals to best navigate the 'Why and How' pathway for the delivery of excellence in care.

Having read the book, at whatever level from the most junior to the most senior leadership roles in delivering care, I would urge you to join the 'Why and How' pathway in pursuit of excellence in care delivery; knowing that the highest quality of care has been delivered is the most compelling stimulus, leading to patient, organisational and self-satisfaction.

Denise has opened a very important way forward for the development of future leaders for which I add my personal thanks.

Baroness Emerton
January 2016

Preface

When I read the public inquiry into the Mid Staffordshire Hospital which described accounts of poor healthcare, high death rates and a bullying culture I was left with many unanswered questions. The first question being why did this happen and the second being how was this allowed to happen in an NHS which is considered to be the best and most envied system in the world?

I have worked for the NHS since 1975, starting my career as a cleaner in the A&E department in the evenings and weekends to support myself while I studied for my A Levels, later to become a nursing auxiliary in the then called 'geriatric wards' before being accepted for my nurse training in 1978. I worked as a staff nurse in male surgery, gynaecology, and community before doing my midwifery training, and later adding various academic qualifications, including completing an education degree and becoming a lecturer for nurses and midwives. Having carried out a range of clinical roles, I joined the world of management and have held director of nursing posts in two acute general hospitals before moving to commissioning roles in the strategic health authority and subsequently the National Commissioning Board – NHS England.

During this time I have worked with the best in nursing, midwifery and medicine. I have worked with some of the greatest leaders in the NHS and a very small number of the worst. My reflections over these years is that the majority of healthcare professionals go above and beyond to provide the best care they can. I can recall a time quite recently, during a major snowfall, of nurses walking several miles in the snow to get to work, to relieve other nurses who had already worked a 14-hour day without a break because the night shift hadn't been able to get to work. When the NHS is at its greatest, the doctors, nurses and all other clinicians do what they do best: they put patients first, they go the extra mile, because they care and that is why they chose to do the job.

So what has gone wrong, how did some nurses and doctors become bad, and why do even the good ones stand by silently and allow poor practice to happen and continue unchecked? How can there be pockets of excellence in one ward or department in a hospital and poor care in another and why is there such variation of practice across the NHS? Why have strong leaders in both nursing and medicine appear to have lost their voice? How can we define good leaders and support them to drive a wholesale improvement in quality and safety in the NHS? How could we select the best leaders to lead organisations, departments and wards and how could we monitor the existing leader, encourage the best and take effective action where poor leadership is observed? All of these whys and hows could provide rich fodder for research topics for many years, but unfortunately the need to address these issues won't wait this long.

As I struggled with these unanswered questions, I considered what I could contribute. Could I use my experience, knowledge and networks to give further thoughts and reflections to some of the questions of how this situation has occurred with the aim of capturing a combination of what some of the literature already tells us, together with the experiences of some key leaders in the NHS, and offer some potential solutions?

I was very privileged to be awarded a Florence Nightingale Scholarship in 2013, and what started as a small study of these issues with the aim of publishing an article has turned into this book.

This book is not presented to be the answer, but more as a vehicle to stimulate greater debate, for you to agree or disagree, or provide alternative views. It is particularly aimed at members of the nursing and medical professions who do not always realise just how much power and influence they have, and that they just need to take it and use it wisely to benefit the patients they serve.

Denise Chaffer
January 2016

About the author

Denise Chaffer is a Registered Nurse and Midwife and currently holds the post of Director of Safety and Learning for the NHS Litigation Authority.

She holds a Master's degree in Management and Social Care, a first degree, plus a Higher Education Teaching qualification and is currently in her third year studying for a PhD in healthcare leadership.

She is a professional Clinical Nursing leader with over 15 years' experience, has been an Executive Director of Nursing in two acute trusts, as well as a Director in a PCT commissioning organisation. More recently she was Director of Nursing for North West London Area Team at NHS England as well as being lead for patient safety across the London Region. She has significant experience of working at international, national and regional level within acute and community settings, nursing, midwifery, education, and on major change and reconfiguration initiatives.

Acknowledgements

I would like to thank the Florence Nightingale Foundation whose support has been integral to the creation of this book.

I would also like to thank all of the contributors to this book. Your generosity in giving your time, your insights and experiences has been really appreciated and has helped to provide the opportunity for readers to gain a range of perspectives on leadership across the healthcare system.

This book is dedicated to all the brilliant nurses and doctors who go the extra mile every day for their patients, and to all of the best leaders in healthcare who always put safety and quality care of patients at the heart of everything they do.

Introduction

The last few years have seen a number of scandals relating to health-care in the UK. The recent public inquiry into the Mid Staffordshire Hospital described accounts of poor healthcare, high death rates and a bullying culture. Many of the themes of the Francis Report (2013) are sadly familiar and similar to those seen in previous investigation reports such as Bristol paediatric cardiac services (Kennedy, 2001), learning disability abuse (Department of Health, 2012) and the very serious failings to safeguard children (Laming, 2003). Not surprisingly the media and British public have grappled to comprehend how such things can occur in a national health service that is supposed to be the envy of the world.

These reports raise some important questions as to why the leaders of professionals, and in particular nurses and doctors, would allow poor practice to happen and continue unchecked. It is important to explore how this occurred rather than seek to blame; we can learn from these events and take more effective measures to make sure such scandals never happen again.

Francis (2013) concludes his report by stating that rather than seek to single out and blame individuals for these failings, the focus should be on addressing the systemic failures which allowed them to take place and continue unchecked. This does not sit well with many who believe very strongly that someone needs to be publicly held to account. Commentators on the events of Mid Staffordshire frequently use the terms of accountability, responsibility and blame interchangeably. Francis highlights the very important issue of addressing organisational culture and the need for more effective leadership at every level. However, despite its 290 recommendations (similar in themes to many previous health investigations), it leaves the 'how' of implementation directly in the hands of the future health professionals and executives.

This book is about both the 'why' and the 'how', in the pursuit of excellence and accountability in healthcare leadership at all levels. It is based on the principles which underpin 'good medicine' (and good nursing) and includes detailed assessment, diagnosis, review of the evidence, and the application of the experiences shared by a group of senior successful healthcare leaders. The purpose of this book is to prescribe the most effective treatment for the problems that exist in the leadership of hospitals in the UK today. It has a particular focus on understanding the influence and impact that 'top team' executive leaders have on the delivery of safe and high-quality care at the front line.

This book will take a fresh look at the characteristics, values and behaviours of top leaders occupying executive hospital board positions and examine how these directly influence high-quality frontline care, in particular the functioning of medicine and nursing care delivery.

It highlights the potential adverse effects of dysfunctional leadership in terms of cost, productivity and health outcomes. It also focuses on the importance of appointing the right people for leadership and continually monitoring their impact on the frontline delivery of care.

This book is for all leaders in healthcare, as whether you are a shift leader in a clinical area, a department/directorate leader, a senior executive, a commissioner, or in higher education and research, the way in which you lead your team will have direct impact on the care of your patients.

This following is an outline of the chapters.

- **Chapter 1** looks at some of theories of successful leadership, and includes thinking on what makes organisations succeed or fail, and the features of good and bad leaders.
- **Chapter 2** examines the role of effective leadership in organisational culture.
- **Chapter 3** discusses the importance of knowing the difference between blame and accountability, and the concept of learning organisations.

- **Chapter 4** looks in more detail at some of the problems specific to nursing and medicine leadership and both the context and environment in which they operate. While there is a need to move towards a more collective clinical leadership and avoidance of silo working, the reason this chapter focuses particularly on nursing and medicine is due to the significant leadership roles they currently hold in many organisations.

- **Chapter 5** includes the unique views of a number of highly successful senior healthcare leaders, who have many years of senior level experience in relation to healthcare provision. The purpose of including these very detailed narratives is to draw out their views and experiences, and look at where combining their accounts with some of the theories of health leadership would help in determining where the most appropriate improvements to leadership could be best targeted.

- **Chapter 6** pulls together both the evidence from the literature and the themes arising from the lived experience of these key leaders to complete the diagnosis.

- **Chapter 7** makes a number of recommendations based on both the evidence from some of the theory and the experiences of the key healthcare leaders to help build a more effective leadership of health organisations. It also proposes a framework for both selection and monitoring of a leadership team, with the aim of providing a consistent approach, and one that not only supports the effective recruitment of the best candidates, but also provides early-warning monitoring systems upon which to act.

CHAPTER 1

Theories on the common features of good and bad leadership

LEADERSHIP THEORIES

The subject of leadership theory is complex, and includes a variety of definitions and characteristics. It appears to be an area that has been widely studied but little understood (Bennis & Nanus, 1985). The quality of leadership is frequently commented on in the media these days and the public appear to show less tolerance for leaders' mistakes and foibles (Yankelovich, 1991).

Prior to the 20th century leadership was often described in terms of 'great man theories', in which individuals such as Napoleon Bonaparte, George Washington and even Adolph Hitler are viewed as men who displayed great leadership and shaped history (Van Wart, 2003). Later these theories included 'trait theories' in the belief that these leaders shared a list of psychological characteristics. Debate among theorists such as Argyris (1957)and McMurry (1958) appear to take opposing positions, McMurry perceiving humans to be lazy by nature and needing leading, whereas Argyris argues that people will move naturally towards growth and development, and need to be nurtured and motivated. It would appear that leadership theories can be viewed from two perspectives, one of focusing on directing specific work-related tasks and goals, or alternatively focusing on creating the optimum psychological and social environments in which work can take place.

Understanding the difference between followers and leaders adds a further dimension to explore. Kean and Haycock (2011) suggest the literature on leadership ignores the significant contribution followers make and the important judgements that staff make as to whether to follow a leader or not. Whitlock (2013) believes that effective leaders set direction and enable culture for others to thrive and that 'good' followership is being recognised increasingly as important.

Despite the lack of empirical research to help construct an evidence base for leadership effectiveness (Willcocks, 2012), there is a growing interest in the concept of 'effective leadership' and a number of books have been written on the subject. These provide managers and leaders with advice on how to improve their leadership effectiveness. In addition there is a range of leadership courses, such as provided by the NHS Leadership Academy, which attempt to utilise a variety of theories to underpin their training on what makes an effective leader. It is difficult to determine which theories or research studies underpin these 'self-help books' and this is compounded by limitations on how effectiveness has been studied and measured. The measurements of leadership effectiveness appear to be primarily based on the concept of staff feedback utilising tools such as 360 degree feedback, assessment centres, staff surveys and other methods of feedback. Another approach to measurement of leadership effectiveness can be seen in relation to organisational outcomes, but they may vary in focus depending on the type of industry. For example, for some the measurement may be in terms of profit, or productivity, and this may include customer satisfaction and market share. Some companies, such as Toyota (Liker, 2004) have a major focus on the quality of their product as their key priority and centre their organisation on this goal. Collins (2001) in his research describes successful organisations as those that make a distinctive impact and deliver superior performance over a period of time.

He believes this applies equally to public sector organisations, stating that the key to success is one that is most relative to the organisation's mission and not necessarily focused on just its financial results.

Disillusionment with these models has led to a growth in support for the concept of a distributed model of leadership which views leadership as a more collective social process (Bolden, Wood & Gosling, 2006). Distributed leadership is one where rather than the focus being on one leader, there is a group of leaders that work and lead together rather than through the actions of individuals (Bennett *et al.*, 2003). One of the key features for those advocating the benefits of distributed leadership is one of enhanced engagement with staff (Spillane, 2006; Gronn, 2008). One benefit (MacBeath, 2005) includes selecting the best people and bringing them together to meet a particular leadership need; this can engender greater engagement and collaborative behaviours of staff (Spillane, 2006). Critics such as Young (2009) state that while leadership may be distributed, often the power is not, and is therefore potentially subject to abuse by senior management who while aiming to encourage engagement and inclusivity don't relinquish their power. This can give an illusion of distributed leadership, marketed as wide engagement, which may not be real.

EXPLORING KEY ELEMENTS OF SUCCESSFUL ORGANISATIONS

Internationally there appears to have been a significant shift away from what are perceived as outdated models of leadership of 'top down' hierarchies and imposition of performance targets, performance frameworks and leadership by fear, towards one of greater collaboration, engagement of the workforce and alignment of common purpose (King's Fund, 2011).

Despite the lack of measurable leadership effectiveness theories, some views on the characteristics of successful organisations are fairly consistent, concluding the job of the 'executives' is no longer to command and control, but to 'cultivate and coordinate the actions of others at all levels of the organisation' (Ancona *et al.*, 2007). New models of leadership see 'leaders drive values, values drive behaviours and behaviours drive performance of an organisation. The collective behaviours of an organisation define its culture' (Frankel, Leonard & Denham, 2006).

THE CONTEXT OF THE CURRENT NHS SYSTEM LEADERSHIP

The NHS system is publicly funded and arguably subject to more central control with accountability to a range of stakeholders. There appear to be some common themes on what takes companies from 'good to great' (Collins, 2001) that are relevant to the leadership of the NHS. Debates about whether the features of leadership which apply in the private sector can be applied to the public sector (Parry & Proctor-Thomson, 2003) tend to focus on perceived differences in relation to business's focus on profit, competition and productivity, and views held that organisations funded by the taxpayer are very different. The NHS in particular has been resistant to the application of the business model, and to the ideological swings of various governments around the need to introduce a market model. For example, there was the Sainsbury style of business seen in the 1980s introduced by the Thatcher Government. The Labour Government, although often perceived as against a business model for running the NHS, introduced during their last term the concept of 'any willing provider', which allowed the contracting out of NHS services to the private sector. The NHS chief executive since 2014 was previously the chief executive of a large US private healthcare organisation and a key author of the NHS plan for Alan Milburn (Secretary of State for Health 1999–2003), which was introduced when the previous Labour Government came into power. It would seem the arguments have become somewhat less polarised regarding the use of the market and competition to drive up quality, and both of the main parties continue to adhere to the overarching principle of healthcare in UK being free at the point of delivery.

One common theme emerging in relation to the public sector is the need for greater adaptability and flexibility, and openness to change. Valle (1999) argues that for the public sector to survive it must be able to mitigate 'perceived stress, decreased personal satisfaction, increase absenteeism and turnover'. The evidence in relation to health appears to suggest good leadership needs to be about engagement and relationship building, devolved and decentralised (Bohmer, 2012).

Collins (2001) in his book *Good to Great*, believes the keys to success are those things most relative to the organisation's mission, and not its financial results.

Successful health organisations share many of these necessary features and while it could be argued these theories don't necessarily apply to the public sector (King's Fund, 2011), there are others that dispute this and fully support the need to embrace these newer theories of leadership.

NHS executive team members commonly hold Master's degrees including MBAs or similar level qualifications in management in the UK, and they are familiar with much of the management theory which defines components of successful management and effective leadership. However, accounts by staff of bullying cultures across some of the leadership of the NHS begs the question of why more leaders don't use the theories they have learnt, instead of focusing more on the 'just get it done mentality'. Many of the media reports on the events at Mid Staffordshire Hospital describe a leadership culture of fear driven by achievement of government targets at all costs, an approach far removed from that recommended by the various theories on effective leadership.

The theory–practice gap is a concept familiar to clinical health professionals, particularly when applied to the clinical setting. Many have adjusted their practice over time to something considerably different to that taught in the classroom. How much of this learning is applied to the practice of leadership poses an interesting question. The application of theory to the selection and monitoring of executive leaders appears to be a less researched area. There have been many attempts to address the performance of executive leadership and these include: executive development determined by Monitor for aspiring foundation trusts; King's Fund programmes; the NHS Leadership Academy leadership and talent management programmes; the NHS Institute; and the National Patient Safety Agency, to name but a few. All were designed to support health professionals in leadership and promote greater understanding of improvement systems and principles of learning organisations. There have been many programmes run over the years to support clinical leadership, such as Leading Empowered Organisations (LEO), Clinical Leaders Network, and the British Association of Medical Managers (BAMM), which appear more recently to have lost momentum, and in the case of BAMM is no longer operating.

The NHS has identified a number of leadership competencies for its top leaders and while setting the standard is a good first step, experience suggests that considerable variation of standards exists across NHS hospitals. The King's Fund commissioned work on the state of NHS leadership and concluded there was a need for a more consistent approach (King's Fund, 2011). They stopped short of recommending a regulatory framework for NHS executives, instead suggesting that NHS leadership culture be subject to greater scrutiny by the existing regulatory bodies such as the Care Quality Commission (CQC) and Monitor. The King's Fund also concluded that the NHS had more in common with the private sector than is often recognised.

Greater attention needs to be given to the selection and monitoring of top teams, and the development of top leaders needs to be mindful of the new models which have a culture of shared leadership. The NHS Leadership Academy was established to deliver a number of programmes, but Bolden *et al.* (2006) argue that future learning needs to be far more work- and team-based for it to achieve effective leadership at all levels.

KEY CHARACTERISTICS OF SUCCESSFUL HEALTHCARE PROVIDERS

Top performing hospitals in the United States show those that made the biggest leaps in terms of healthcare value, safety, quality and customer value had a number of common features. A sample of the top four hospitals studied showed achievements of top scores in quality of care while keeping use of resources low. The most common feature was that hospital leaders had set clear goals for the organisations and aligned daily practice to these objectives. Frankel, Leonard and Denham (2006) showed that leadership by an organisation's trustees, chief executives and physician leaders was seen as the single most important success factor in reducing barriers and making performance improvement and transformation. Senior leaders in most of the well-respected organisations had been in their posts for many years, and when they did leave they were often replaced by long-serving leaders from within the organisations, unlike the NHS where chief executives' tenure is often limited to under 18 months (Santry, 2007, citing Bohmer, 2012). Other interesting aspects of successful top teams is the inclusion of a higher percentage of women on boards; in many examples this has significantly enhanced overall performance of the organisations studied (King's Fund, 2011).

The commonality between the successful health organisations includes pursuing quality and access, and shows that cost reduction is a consequence not the primary goal of their efforts. They all reinforced goals by addressing organisational culture and implementing a culture of continuous quality improvement.

The Institute for Healthcare Improvement (IHI), which has wide international membership, defined their core mission (described as the triple aim) as to:

- improve the health of the nation
- enhance the patient experience of care, including quality, access and reliability
- reduce, or at least control, the per capita cost of care.

The triple aim is included in hospitals across the United States, where the strategy has been widely embraced and a renewed focus by hospital boards is driving quality to reduce costs, with a specific focus on reduction of waste.

One impressive output of this initiative was seen at the Auckland IHI conference in 2012, which had a high level of attendance from senior clinicians. Many of them gave keynote addresses and ran workshops about clinicians taking the lead and accepting accountability for the quality of the care delivered. An interesting aspect of the conference was the collaboration between clinicians and chief executives, with shared vision for their organisations committed to the triple aim.

There is some evidence which links high staff satisfaction in NHS hospitals with higher patient satisfaction and also with feeling valued by management; there are also links to meaningful appraisals and feeling involved (King's Fund, 2011). The variables that currently exist in drawing conclusions from national patient and staff surveys are complex, together with the sample size, and there is potential for bias in motivation for staff and patients to return questionnaires. The Care Quality Commission collects data known as the 'intelligent monitoring tool' from each trust, bringing together a number of measures and scoring systems which are publicly available. It is difficult to draw meaningful conclusions from much of this data. However, many of these quality measures, which have been used by hospitals in England for some time, should have highlighted the 'red flags' which were present in detecting the many failings on the scale seen in the Mid Staffordshire Hospital. The trust had high mortality rates, and there was local public concern in the form of complaints and media stories. What is unclear is why the board failed to act, and an understanding of the extent to which they were aware of how much an outlier this trust actually was. This poses the question of whether there is a better and more evidence-based way of predicting potential failure which takes a more integrated approach to an organisation and sits at the heart of the functioning of the executive team.

KEY CHARACTERISTICS OF FAILING ORGANISATIONS

There have been a number of highly publicised failings of health organisations leading to increased patient mortality, such as Maidstone and Tunbridge Wells NHS Trust (Mid Staffordshire Hospital), and poor care delivery. What is common to these failings is a tendency to seek blame (and shame) sometimes aimed at a particular profession, in particular nursing. Often a scatter gun approach is taken to identify the cause, concluding it must be the training, or the selection, as to why we have such poor nurses. Sometimes the blame is aimed at a particular chief executive and as a knee-jerk action they may be removed in a very public way. While executives should be held accountable, as they and their boards are responsible for the governance of their organisation, there is a need for greater understanding of the difference between blame and accountability. This is critical to achieving effective leadership and changing organisational culture. Frequently action plans are rapidly developed in response to a large number of external bodies' view of what may be the organisation's problems. There needs to be a full, comprehensive diagnosis and analysis of the true root cause and context of the failings to ensure that action plans explicitly relate to the areas they are seeking to address.

The outputs from failing organisations are fairly obvious. In the non-public sector this relates to falling profits, financial loss, and rapid turnover of staff, failure to attract and recruit good people, and poor quality products that are not demanded. In the NHS, organisations are measured across a number of key performance indicators, usually including financial, access targets, compliance to regulatory standards, and a range of safety and quality outcomes. Commonly NHS trusts are ranked from best to worst across a number of these benchmarks, and variations between hospitals are publicly available. The limitation of this approach is that in every measure using comparisons there will be a best, a worst and a number in the middle. This is best illustrated in the national patient survey results, where a trust can be labelled as either the best or worst in the country. This in turn attracts much 'brow beating' and generation of action plans, without being clear what really is the actual benchmark, and more importantly what is the cause of the problem. Instead trusts tend to make a guess at the cause and produce a number of actions to try to make the necessary improvements. Typically where this doesn't secure the improvements needed, the result is falling staff morale and a lack of confidence in the organisation.

Rather than wait for organisations to fail, it would be more helpful to accurately detect early signs of potential failings. Collins (2000), citing Tomlinson (2012) provides a useful framework to help to do this. Based on research over 5 years of failing companies, he identified five stages of decline which lead organisations to failure. These include: hubris born of success; undisciplined pursuit of more; denial of risk and peril; grasping for salvation; and capitulation to irrelevance or death.

Hubris

Hubris is a term derived from the Greek meaning 'inviting disaster as well as arrogance' and denotes overconfidence where a person in a position of power can be 'so convinced they are right' (Owen, 2008). Application of this to the NHS can be seen where organisations view themselves as 'superior' and deserving of their position. This can sometimes be observed in some large teaching hospitals who may see themselves as successful more for what they stand for and their history than what they are actually delivering. Where this occurs the leadership may deny or neglect external threats, ignore feedback, lose perspective on what is their core business and cease to function as a learning organisation. They may also attribute their previous success entirely to their perceived 'supreme leadership' rather to one of luck and history.

Undisciplined pursuit of more

Where the organisation fails to understand its weaknesses and overestimates its success, it may move to make 'undisciplined leaps' to become bigger and acquire other organisations. Collins (2001) describes this as 'over reaching' and it can occur when the organisation fails to employ the right people in its leadership positions. Organisations can see acquisitions as a way to increase income rather than install discipline to address underlying financial challenges. Examples can be seen of this in the NHS where failing organisations look to mergers with another to resolve their problems; this may include simply taking on more services, such as community provision, or a full merger with another hospital that may have very similar problems. There can be a loss of reality in the leaders, who are seeking more in terms of personal interests and position over the needs of the organisation.

Denial of risk and peril

In stage three, leaders start to discount negative data (Collins, 2001), they exaggerate positive data, and start to blame external factors for their problems. They refuse to hear bad news or negative reports from both inside and outside the organisation and focus on a degree of 'spin' rather than reality. This was very well illustrated in the case of Mid Staffordshire Hospital where the accountable leadership at all levels sought to disagree with and defend data that clearly pointed to the problems that existed. There tends to be a reliance on reassurance versus assurance, where boards seek reassurances about issues rather than insisting on robust triangulated evidence to support the level of risk. Usually there is a decline in healthy dialogue and debate and a shift towards autocratic management. Staff then resort to telling the 'executives' more of what they think they want to hear than the facts and tend to keep 'bad news' from them.

Sometimes rather than confront the difficulties and their root cause, institutions embark on organisational restructures, believing these will resolve their problems. Staff get increasingly involved in internal politics, while the executives distance themselves and increasingly disconnect from their staff.

Grasping for salvation

At this stage the solution is often to go and seek a saviour, a 'charismatic visionary leader' (Collins, 2001) to save the organisation. Unfortunately this rarely works as the new leader brings in 'new programmes' or 'new strategies' to try to motivate and mobilise the workforce. This is frequently seen in the NHS where there is a belief that a new chief executive or chief operating director will be the key to 'turning organisations around'. There is usually an initial burst of positive outputs, but because the top team has failed to address its real problems confusion and cynicism set in. Where staff are unable to articulate the organisation's core values, or worse they have been written by the top team and imposed, staff become mistrustful, regarding 'visions' and PR as nothing more than rhetoric. The chronic restructuring makes the financial situation worse and staff become less productive.

Capitulation to irrelevance or death

Stage 5 is described by Collins as fatal; at this point leaders give up, leave (or are removed), or as is the case within the NHS, chief executives are removed or the organisation faces the failure regime being applied.

These stages of decline provide a helpful tool in helping to diagnose the root causes that drive NHS failings, and provide a framework for early detection of these stages and to plan interventions to avoid reaching stage 5. There are a number of interventions that can be applied at each stage to reverse the stages of decline but this requires the presence of effective leadership to be able to implement a sustainable strategy for success.

CHARACTERISTICS OF SUCCESSFUL ORGANISATIONS AND EFFECTIVE LEADERSHIP

Determining the extent to which leaders can be viewed as effective and their impact on the success of an organisation is problematic because it is highly dependent on what is understood by the term 'effective' and whether the outcomes of 'impact on success' are both external and internal. These outcomes can include anything from financial performance and profits to production or delivery of a 'quality product'.

Some studies conclude that leadership of highly successful organisations includes a number of common features, one of which is that chief executive officers (CEOs) of great companies are largely anonymous, and there is an absence of a 'celebrity CEO'. Also, the leader's ambition is for the greatness of the work and the company, rather than for themselves (Collins, 2000). These leaders have the confidence to surround themselves with great people (Drucker, 2003). There is a need for humility as the antidote to charisma, and successful leadership must be based upon the fundamentals of values, ethics and accountability. Leaders must have the confidence to recognise their own limitations and hire the right people to plug the gap (Maynard, 2005). The King's Fund (2011) argues for 'no more heroes', reflecting on the common response of parachuting in a 'saviour chief executive' to save and turn around failing organisations.

Good leadership needs to be about engagement and relationship building, devolved and decentralised. The chief executives need to establish clinical leadership at every level and this requires trust and the confidence to support and coach rather than control and command (Robert Naylor interviewed: *see* Bohmer, 2012). This can be difficult when there can be directives from the centre (i.e. government) that can conflict with devolution. The introduction of clinical commissioning groups has continued to test this tension as they become more confident in their role, where the government has introduced legislation to support delegation to what they describe as frontline clinicians (GPs), and it will be interesting to observe how much control the NHS leadership system asserts in terms of providing assurance to the centre.

The *Financial Times* reported in 2006 (cited by Owen, 2008) the habits of highly ineffective prime ministers, many of which could also be applied to leaders of NHS organisations. They include:

- failure to lead collegiate administration
- failure to manage expenditure
- failure to follow through
- adoption of heroic CEO model
- top-down leadership
- failure to listen to criticism
- addiction to targets and performance measures
- lack of stable organisation surroundings.

In terms of the findings from the events of Mid Staffordshire many of these can be seen to have been present, and could equally apply to both the previous and current governments. Studies of political leaders conclude similar observations in terms of effective leadership. Owen (2008) records the leadership features of a number of world leaders. For example, George W. Bush (US President 2001–9) reported 'he would appoint the right people, delegate authority and hold them to account for results', but unfortunately these were not actions that were later seen to be displayed in practice. Owen believes some of political leaders studied developed 'hubris syndrome', where they become so convinced they are right that they show a lack of interest and even display contempt for others who may know better. Owen describes both George Bush and Tony Blair as developing signs of 'hubris syndrome' and highlights their excessive confidence, restlessness, inattention to detail, and focus on 'presentism'. This he believes was taken to excess with Blair during the Iraq War (from 2003) where a central command and control stance was taken with a discreet 'inner circle' making all the decisions at the perceived exclusion of the department leads who would have been better placed to advise.

Owen described hubris syndrome as one that develops in leaders over a period of time. Whether this can be included as a formal psychiatric disorder is not yet established. Owen, in acknowledging this, believes this syndrome needs to be seriously considered as where hubris is present in its leader, an organisation will ultimately face decline and failure.It is an interesting question whether it is possible to predict which individuals being selected for leadership positions may develop hubris. Many readers will be familiar with an individual who gets promoted and the power seems to go to their head. Nurses will be familiar with the situation in which some newly qualified staff nurses develop a syndrome commonly described by their juniors as 'staffitis'; similarly junior doctors work with a number of consultants with different leadership styles which will ultimately shape the type of doctors they may become. The stereotype of the consultants depicted in the *Carry On Doctor* comedy films of the 1960s can still be found in some hospitals today.

Organisations may also encounter other types of dysfunctional leaders, covering a range of personality disorders, and including 'psychopaths' 'sociopaths', and those with 'narcissistic' traits (Clarke, 2005). Common features of all are unethical behaviours, intolerance, superficial charm, unpredictable behaviours, workplace bullying, embellishment of own achievements, and individuals driven by admiration.

It appears that individuals with these traits can be repeatedly promoted to positions of leadership (Pech & Slade, 2007), possibly due to their ability to embellish and manipulate their way past even the most robust recruitment and selection processes. This may be further compounded by organisations when they detect potential failure and look to select a 'charismatic leader or outside saviour' who they believe can come in and rescue the organisation (Collins 2001, citing Tomlinson, 2012). They may inadvertently appoint a leader with a personality disorder or with a propensity to develop hubris syndrome who regards their success as an entitlement.

Responsibility for avoiding appointing dysfunctional leaders and removing those that start to display these characteristics ultimately lies with the non-executives and the chairman of NHS trust boards, many of whom may not be effectively equipped to deal with this syndrome. This may be complicated by the charismatic style of behaviour that may have endeared these individuals to a small number of the executive team and hospital staff.

Outdated views of leadership can include those that believe that rule by fear and enforced compliance gets the best results and where the organisation has sought an individual to address failings there may be support for what is seen as a 'strong leadership style'; for example, support for 'coming down hard on those responsible for poor care'. This view is also supported by Glaser (2006) who sees compliance as an outmoded strain of DNA based upon a belief that leaders need to control what others do; strategy gets implemented from the top and you get 'buy in' by demanding it. The evidence is that leading through fear and blame will lead to overall failure of the organisation and staff will seek to avoid conflict, keep

1. Position: people follow because they have to
2. Permission: people follow because they want to
3. Production: people follow because of what you have done for the organisation
4. People Development: people follow because of what you have done for them
5. Pinnacle: people follow because of what you represent

FIGURE 1.1 Maxwell's (2011) five levels of leadership

their heads down and make sure bad news is kept away from the executive team for fear of the possible consequences.

Maxwell (2011) provides a useful framework for diagnosing levels of effective leadership. He classifies 'positional power' as the lowest rating (level 1), where people follow because they have to. He states how commonly level 1 leaders find it impossible to work with level 3 and 4 leaders; they are frequently either moved on or removed, and sometimes their careers end as the level 1 leader is unable to work with those they believe to be a threat to their position. Maxwell claims that where level 1 leaders are appointed as executives, this will inevitably lead to the organisation's failure. Maxwell's theory for defining levels of leadership provides a useful framework for designing a tool to support both the selection and monitoring of those in executive leadership positions. These include defining five levels of leadership (*see* Figure 1.1).

Maxwell's work is very helpful in defining each level and his excellent book *The 5 Levels of Leadership* provides self-assessment for leaders to examine their own level and see how they can become more effective leaders.

There are a number of strategies that boards may consider for their development, which include 360 degree feedback for the board members, executive away day developmental days, and bringing in external consultants. Boards need to be mindful of the manipulation that dysfunctional leaders are capable of and their ability to control others by fear, who may feel unable to speak out as they dread consequences.

It can be seen that the concept of effective leadership is complex and subject to a variety of definitions, which makes it very difficult to measure. In addition, terms of effective leadership and change culture are frequently used interchangeably in describing ambitions to improve the NHS. The next chapter explores further the concept of organisational culture and its relationship to leadership.

CHAPTER 2

Exploring the relationship of effective leadership to organisational culture

Defining organisational culture appears to be an elusive concept. Francis (2013) speaks about the need to address organisational culture and the need to radically change the culture of the NHS. Changing culture is a not a simple process and culture can be difficult to describe and measure. Most know what a 'bad culture' feels like, in particular where there are reports of bullying cultures or low staff morale.

There are a range of views on the extent leadership is shaped by culture or whether leaders shape cultures. Many attempts by researchers to quantify organisational culture and culture change are hindered by lack of empirical models to aid investigation (Silvester, Anderson & Patterson, 1999). Alvesson (1993) argues that organisational culture has come to represent everything and therefore nothing in organisational research. He highlights a fundamental failure of organisational psychologists to consider their epistemological assumptions, which has further served to suppress debate. However, despite the difficulties in agreeing any single definition, many have made attempts. A number of authors present categories or 'typologies' to break culture into more measurable components. Harrison (1972) presents a 'typology' of four main types of culture: power; role; task/achievement; person/support. Cameron and Quinn

(1999) describe another typology which includes: clannish; hierarchical; market-orientated; and adhocratic. These appear to have been adapted over time. This has led to the development of a number of 'cultural measurement tools' against these types of categories which have been used in a range of settings in an attempt to measure culture. The weakness of this approach is that without a commonly accepted definition it is virtually impossible to measure, and a number of these tools may be measuring perception of how the organisation feels, which will vary depending on who is being asked. The tools used in a number of studies include 'team climate inventory' (Bosch et al., 2008), or the 'competing values framework' of Zammuto and Krakower (1991).

Parry and Proctor-Thomson (2003) pose the question of whether 'leadership is a function of culture, or organisational culture is a function of the leadership'. While some suggest that leaders help to create the culture, and in turn shape its members (Hampden-Turner, 1990), others see leadership as a function of culture or alternatively that organisational culture is a function of leadership 'manifested' (Parry & Proctor-Thomson, 2003). On the other hand, it could be argued that culture is a key factor in moderating the relationship between leader, behaviour and leadership effectiveness, (House, 1995). Some theorists conceptualise culture as varying between individualism and collectivism (Kim et al., 2004).

Where the organisational culture is viewed as strong, it is often described as distinctive, and seen as characterised by consensus on beliefs, norms, values and ideals (Robbins, 1996). This strong culture is where the leadership communicates to its staff expectations of how they should behave. Hopkins, Hopkins and Mallette (2005) propose one of the more simple approaches to determining values, identity and behaviours. They describe values as defining what is important to the organisation's identity in relation to what the organisation stands for, and therefore behaviour is defined as the understanding by the organisation of what is and is not acceptable to the organisation. The important relationship of values to changing organisational culture is illustrated by Collins (2000) whose research showed organisations with strong values outperformed the general stock market by a factor of 12 over a period of 70 years. Another study by the Institute of Management and Administration (2002) showed that workers in an organisation with a value-based culture were more likely to be proud to work with their companies and identify them as good places to work. One of the most important features given is the importance of leaders promoting values and to ensure they are seen to be living them.

Bass and Avolio (1993) believe that a transformational style of leadership will impact directly on cultural change and is the most likely to bring about improvement. Some believe the role of employees is to serve the top management (Schein, 1993). Examples of this include, the 'top team' determining the culture and using selection processes to evaluate the fit of individuals to the corporate culture and conducting performance appraisals against the desired culture (Pascale, 1985). The belief is that this serves to benefit the employers, but it is not so clear where the benefits to the employees lie. This strong culture concept is one where there is an imposition of values on the organisation. The 'Functionalist' belief is that culture is and can be subject to control of management and therefore can be created and imposed (Ogbonna & Wilkinson, 2003). Supporters of the imposition of strong cultures believe that an organisation's effectiveness is dependent on the development of strong culture and this will therefore lead to greater employee commitment and improved quality. The belief is that corporate-defined culture will secure 'unusual effort on behalf of apparently ordinary employees' (Peters & Waterman, 1982). Some organisations make a deliberate attempt to adopt a strong culture and include statements about imposed beliefs, norms, values and ideals (Robbins, 1996) These are communicated to employees, informing how they should behave, and the top-down prescribed culture is enforced in various ways (Legge, 1995). Schein (1993) describes this as the practitioner serving top management. Examples include a range of recruitment and appraisal systems that aim to fit the individual to the organisation (Pascale, 1985).

Some argue that organisations which develop a strong culture will have greater employee commitment and improved quality, and that leading and driving a strong corporate culture will secure 'unusual effort on behalf of apparently ordinary employees' (Bagraim, 2001). Others, such as Alvesson (1993) disagree, stating that the imposition of a strong top-down culture is likely to be unsuccessful as it fails to recognise and engage the range of subcultures that exist in any organisation. This approach also raises some potential ethical concerns. Alvesson argues this approach can be seen as manipulation by top management and it denies the importance of individuality. Some culture initiatives commissioned by top management can be viewed by staff as simply made to advance management's own interests. Other commentators (Parry & Proctor-Thomson, 2003) view engagement with staff in the attempt to 'win hearts and minds' as manipulative, and argue that individuality can't survive in an organisation with a strong culture that sets values norms and doesn't allow an individual to choose between sets of values. The risk is that strong cultures may lead to staff feigning belief in the organisation's ideology as necessary to obtain organisational needs (Bagraim, 2001). This is illustrated by Ogbonna and Wilkinson (2003) who undertook a case study of middle managers in grocery retailing; while this is outside of the health setting some parallels can be drawn. The study has the strategic importance of managing organisational culture as its central theme, and aimed to measure the impact of an introduced culture change on managers in a supermarket chain. A previous study had looked at behaviour of shop floor workers. The researchers utilised three data sources which included documents related to the organisation's imposed strategy, observation of managerial behaviour in a range of settings and in-depth face-to-face semi-structured interviews (30 interviews with 15 managers). Their conclusions questioned whether the changes to managers' leadership behaviours are in fact related far more to surveillance, direct control and threat of sanctions than any change of managerial values and organisational change. They conclude that the imposition of 'organisational culture' as a method for organisations to improve performance through transforming values is a 'false promise' which is presented as a superior, 'cheaper form of control than bureaucratic; it is in fact instrumental compliance'. The relevance of this study is that its conclusions don't reject the aim of changing the ways in which staff behave, but do reject that this results in a 'change of culture'. This is well illustrated within their study where the imposed 'culture change' by management was to make the frontline checkout staff be nicer to the customers. The result was that they did improve staff interactions with customers, but they didn't change their view of customers. The researchers conclude that even though the strategy changed behaviour it didn't change 'hearts and minds'.

Parallels can be drawn with the 2013 Chief Nurse '6 Cs strategy', which is based on the assumption that a top-down strategy will address the leadership and cultural problems highlighted by Francis (2013). The strategy was led by the chief nurse for England, with the aim to get nurses to be more 'compassionate'. Other initiatives included recruiting for values, and closer monitoring of compassionate and caring behaviours. The question this leads to is whether it would be possible to design and develop a strategy to improve the culture of healthcare delivery as currently being proposed post Francis. It appears that, while being actively promoted, the concept of effective leadership as a vehicle to drive culture change in the NHS fails to acknowledge the lack of understanding of how this can be achieved and that any robust evidence to support it being either measurable or achievable is at best limited.

Despite the difficulties of defining culture, many would argue that they feel they are able to detect or 'feel' signs of a weak corporate culture when they walk into organisations. An example may be where there is no clear statement of values or there are too many or there is lack of agreement with them. The executives may contradict the values in their actions and style of leadership; for example, leaders may communicate the message that quality products or service is important but at the same time be implementing cost-cutting strategies including training cuts (Hopkins, Hopkins & Mallette, 2005). There may be hostility to leadership from staff, and no common sharing of values throughout the organisation.

Hospitals, like all other organisations, have by their very nature a number of subcultures. Examples of these include the various professional groups, support services, different racial and religious groups, and gender. Understanding the varying subcultures and the various interdependencies within an organisation, which help unite individuals and foster a common set of values and beliefs, takes skilled leadership. Unless unity is achieved subcultures will pull in different directions and these subcultures are often underestimated at the leader's peril. While many trusts have made significant progress on equality and diversity agendas, very few have truly analysed and addressed the wide range of values that may exist across their staff groups.

Many commentators on the NHS continue to advocate the need to 'change the culture', or argue that the culture is the problem. The culture of NHS organisations continues to represent what is known as a 'wicked issue' and requires a far greater depth of definition, understanding and agreement of what the positive outcome measurement may be. It is not something that can be effectively addressed with a top-down approach such as directing staff to be more compassionate. The following chapter explores the concept of 'safety culture' and considers approaching the need to change culture from the perspective of development of a learning organisation (Senge, 1990).

CHAPTER 3

Understanding the difference between blame and accountability, and applying learning organisation principles

With a contribution from Dr Suzette Woodward*

'*The single greatest impediment to error prevention is that we punish people for making mistakes.*'

(Leape, 2009)

* Dr Suzette Woodward has worked for over 20 years in patient safety, from being a patient safety manager in a frontline organisation in the NHS to working at national level at the Department of Health, National Patient Safety Agency and the NHS Litigation Authority. Suzette is a paediatric intensive care nurse who has a doctorate in Patient Safety and an MSc in Clinical Risk. She is currently the National Campaign Director for the Sign up to Safety campaign for the NHS in England, which aims to save lives and reduce avoidable harm. Suzette has been nominated by her peers via the *Health Service Journal* as one of the top inspirational women in the NHS in 2013, a top nursing leader in 2014 and a top clinical leader in 2015.

INTRODUCTION

The response to the Francis report (2013) provides an interesting illustration of the confusion between blame and accountability, and sees various commentators demanding that those they feel to blame should be removed from office. The rationale is that 'someone must to be held to account' for events such as those that occurred at Mid Staffordshire NHS Foundation Trust. Comparisons are made with the private sector, indicating that where such an overwhelming failure has occurred chief executives or whole boards would be removed. There has since been an increasing trend towards directors within the NHS being removed from their posts following significant failings, both after the events of Mid Staffordshire and in circumstances where trusts have been seen to have significant failings following CQC inspections.

The public also expects that individuals who are personally and directly accountable for the delivery of what was described as 'appalling care' would be held to account by both the organisation and their regulatory bodies. There were also many more staff that could be found guilty by 'acts of omission' in terms of their professional failure to act, standing by as witnesses of poor care and doing nothing about it. There will be others at all levels, too, that were constrained by the system to speak up for fear of the consequences, or lacked the courage to articulate the unintended consequences of blindly following top-down targets, and by doing so put patient lives at risk. Somewhere in this process of pursuit of particular targets the intent became grossly distorted and the patients' best interests were lost and in some cases significant harm was caused. This chapter explores the difference between blame and accountability, alongside discussion of the need to develop a learning organisation and a 'just culture'.

The terms blame and accountability are often used interchangeably. The word accountability is widely misused (Brenner, 2005). To be accountable means to be responsible for and answerable for an activity. If something goes wrong, those accountable are expected to answer for their part in the goings on, because of the need for their knowledge to correct systems. It is important to gain the knowledge to prevent future failings; those accountable often have useful information. Blame is associated with punishment and therefore fear should not be a factor in seeking those accountable.

Brenner (2005) defines a number of ways that blame and accountability differ, and states that if individual blame is the goal, potential for learning stops when 'the culprits' have been found. Also, if fear of accountability is present, this suggests staff are operating in a 'blame culture'. If those found accountable are at the bottom of an organisational structure, the chances are that blame is a feature, as in the majority of cases safety incidents will have arisen due to a combination of events including wider system failure.

When discussing safety in healthcare, reference is often made to replicating the successes of the aviation industry. Changes in aviation came about as a result of a number of high-profile crashes which resulted in the death of a great number of passengers. The investigations found that the contributory factors associated with these disasters included: teams and how they worked together; the ability of a junior member of the team to speak out to a more senior member of the team; and the view that the pilot 'knew best'. What the airline industry has now demonstrated is that while the pilot has overall accountability for the lives on board, these pilots work within a system. The subsequent safety programme that followed these events has seen a significant improvement in the safety record in most parts of the aviation industry.

The point Francis makes on accountability for the events of Mid Staffordshire are similar to the approach taken by Professor James Reason (1997), in that where there is an overwhelming organisational system failure, and where accountability is held at many levels, singling out one individual to blame would not address the root cause of the system failure.

PRINCIPLES OF THE LEARNING ORGANISATION CONCEPT

In his speech of 16 July 2015, Secretary of State for Health Jeremy Hunt stated an ambition for the NHS to become the 'world's largest learning organisation' (Department of Health, 2015). Senge (1990, p. 3) defines learning organisations as ones where 'people continually expand their capacity to create the results they truly desire, where new and expansive patterns of thinking are nurtured, where collective aspiration is set free, and where people are continually learning to see the whole together'. Applying these principles to top team leaders gives the responsibility to executives to establish the context for the organisation, shape the culture and establish the organisational ethics (Berwick, 2012). By ethics, Berwick means the responsibility of organisations to promote quality, reduce harm and reduce waste. The context relates to the whole organisation and that in which it operates. Senge's work focuses on system-wide thinking, and the need to bring human values to the workplace, the need to understand the connectivity of the various parts of the organisation, and how by decentralising the role of leadership we enhance the capacity of all people to work productively to meet common goals.

The principles of a 'learning organisation' see all staff as learners and that the concept of system-wide thinking is critical to help staff understand the context in which they work. Where there are failures to understand such systems the result can be blaming of individuals without recognising the context in which staff operate. Senge's system thinking has underpinned the approach to incident management in recent times. Francis (2013) is clear in his report in stating that rather than seeking to single out and blame individuals for these failings, the focus should be on addressing the system failures which allowed them to take place and continue unchecked. Unfortunately this is not necessarily the experience of many of the staff delivering care in the NHS and there continues to be considerable lack of understanding of the important differences between blame, just culture and accountability. This in turn has led to wider variations between NHS settings in the position they take on disciplining staff for patient safety issues.

To move all NHS trusts to become learning organisations requires a new type of leadership. Senge (1990) describes leaders as designers, stewards and teachers whose responsibility is to build an organisation where staff continually expand their capabilities and share the vision.

Seeing top team leaders as learners is supported by the work of Ancona *et al.* (2007) who highlight the importance of acknowledging the concept of the 'incomplete leader'. Their work dispels the myth that leaders have expertise in all areas they need to lead an organisation, and recognises that the executive job is no longer to command and control but to cultivate and coordinate the actions of others. Not all organisations will have the expertise needed to improve safety, but the 'incomplete leaders' know when to let go and understand that leadership exists throughout the organisation. They can appoint those around them to plug the gaps of knowledge required, which in turn helps them lead the organisation.

A learning organisation is one that identifies the system factors which affect patient safety and one that supports an increase in the reliability of the processes within their organisation. The aim is to improve this reliability by:

- prevention: designing the system to prevent failure
- identification: making failures obvious before they occur by undertaking proactive risk assessments
- mitigation: designing the procedures and building capabilities for mitigating harm caused by the failures when they are not detected or intercepted.

There is variability in safety and reliability approaches, something which can be measured in at least two ways. First, the CQC in their hospital inspections analysis produce a range of data known as 'Hospital Intelligent Monitoring' which can be viewed on the CQC website (www.cqc.org.uk). This includes the triangulation of data across a range of measures, and in particular the national staff survey's response to whether they feel able to report incidents, and the current levels of external safety reporting via the National Reporting and Learning System (NRLS). A second additional measure is the data collected by royal colleges and trade unions on the percentage of staff disciplined for safety incidents. The Royal College of Nursing represents nurses across the UK and reports wider variations in practice (for example, how a nurse is treated when there is a drug error); this data could be more widely shared with the aim of reducing this variability of approach. The Royal College of Midwives published a study (Leversidge, 2012) which showed the disproportionate percentage of black and minority ethnic midwives (over 60%) that were going through disciplinary processes in London, demonstrating the urgent need for this to be addressed.

THE BALANCED APPROACH TO SAFETY

It is generally accepted within the field of healthcare that the majority of safety incidents are due to a system failure of some kind. The systems approach to safety acknowledges that the causes of a patient safety incident cannot simply be linked to the actions of the individual healthcare staff involved. All incidents are also linked to the system in which the individuals were working. Looking at what was wrong in the system helps organisations to learn lessons that can prevent the incident recurring.

The NHS has focused on encouraging the reporting of incidents, the investigation of serious incidents and developing action plans. Generally the reporting of incidents has increased as organisations have been encouraged to ensure learning from incidents. However, an inherent risk of this approach can be too great a focus on the process of reporting and investigating incidents rather than on ensuring and assuring the learning is taking place and future incidents are being prevented. In addition there can be an over-generation of multiple action plans, with less attention to the monitoring of their impact.

Commercial industries such as oil and gas have a culture in which it is not accepted that incidents are inevitable and not preventable. They apply a position of zero tolerance to incidents, which focuses them more specifically on the root cause. These root causes inevitably fall into categories of the need to make a change in behaviour, procedure or material. They advocate shifting the focus from reporting and processing incidents to one of mastering the study of 'near misses', which they believe provide the best intelligence in prevention and learning, and implementing predictive techniques to reduce harm. This approach is wholly compatible with learning from system failure and understanding human factors, but with far greater focus on taking the action needed to rectify the situation and reduce risk.

Proactive learning and improving patient safety depend upon a culture where we learn from our mistakes, whether they be near misses or incidents that result in actual harm. It is through the lessons of our everyday errors that we can design our environment to be less error prone and more error tolerant.

A safety culture is where staff within an organisation have a constant and active awareness of the potential for things to go wrong. Both the staff and management are able to acknowledge mistakes, learn from them, and take action to put things right. However, there is a misunderstanding in the NHS that a safety culture is one that is 'blame free'. This is not the case now and has never been the case. In all policy documents and guidance since 2000 (Department of Health, 2000; NPSA 2004), the expected culture has always been described as 'open and fair', where staff are treated fairly but also held accountable for their actions. This is vital for both the safety of patients and the well-being of those who provide their care.

A fundamental part of any organisation with a culture of safety is to ensure that is it open and fair. For NHS organisations this means that:

- staff are open about incidents they have been involved in
- staff and organisations are accountable for their actions
- staff feel able to talk to their colleagues and superiors about any incident
- NHS organisations are open with patients, the public and staff when things have gone wrong, and explain what lessons will be learned
- staff are treated fairly and supported when an incident happens.

The Department of Health's publication, *An Organisation with a Memory* (DoH, 2000), highlighted how up until that point the NHS had operated in a culture of blame rather than promoting openness. When things went wrong the response was often to seek one or two frontline workers to blame. They in turn may have faced disciplinary measures or professional censure and media attention. The National Audit Office report (2003) on suspensions of clinical staff following patient safety incidents also found that several staff were suspended despite evidence of systemic failures rather than individual shortcomings.

The Kennedy Report (2001) recommended that every effort should be made to create an open and non-punitive environment in the NHS in which it is safe to report and admit incidents. Subsequent governments have since made it clear that being open and fair must become a top priority in healthcare. In his speech of 16 July 2015 (DoH, 2015), Secretary of State for Health Jeremy Hunt went further, stating his belief that 'a no blame learning culture' in the airline industry has led to drastic reductions in both fatalities and cost, and the need to achieve the same in healthcare.

THE CONCEPT OF 'JUST CULTURE'

Over the last 15 years the term 'open and fair culture' has been replaced by the term 'just culture' (Dekker, 2007; Marx, 2009). A just culture is a helpful way of explaining a safety culture that includes accountability and distinguishes the following subcategories:

- human error and repeated human error
- risky behaviour and violations
- negligence
- reckless behaviour.

The just culture for safety recommends that staff involved in human error are supported and consoled; staff who are demonstrating risky behaviour should be asked why before being judged; and staff who are reckless in their behaviour (i.e. they have a conscious disregard for their patients' and colleagues' safety) should be disciplined appropriately.

Human error

Human error is defined as inadvertent action or inadvertently doing other than what should have been done. The error is often described as a slip, lapse or mistake. These are common to everyone, and we all make mistakes because of a brief lapse in concentration or forgetfulness or due to stress. We are easily distracted, or unfocused, leading to an increased propensity to error. The important fact, though, is that human error is unintentional, accidental and unplanned. There is no intent to be erroneous – therefore the response should not be to discipline. The appropriate response is to support and console.

Repeated human error

Some hospitals report that they will take disciplinary actions against staff if there is a repeated error, such as nurses involved in repeated medication errors. However, repeat error could be due to a number of conditions and not because the nurse or other professional is more erroneous than others; the type of activity, the contextual environment, the culture of the unit or the complexity of the patient or task may cause individuals to have a higher propensity to error or in fact individuals who have erred before can be more likely to do it again because of the stress caused by the previous error.

Risky behaviour

Risky behaviour is exhibited when someone makes a behavioural choice that has the potential to increase risk. For example, this may be due to the risk not being recognised or mistakenly believed to be justified. Risky behaviour can include violations (non-adherence to policy) and/or negligence. Examples of this are knowingly not following standard procedures and guidelines (which require or prohibit a set of behaviours).

Violations of or not adhering to guidelines can be for a number of reasons. They can be either unintentional rule violations or intentional rule violations.

- **Unintentional violation:** this is usually when the individual was not aware of the rule or did not understand it, or it was not clear or was hidden in some way.
- **Intentional violation:** this often occurs when an individual chooses to knowingly violate a rule while performing a task – but crucially does not necessarily mean they were doing so to the detriment of their patients' safety.

An example of risk taking or violation that may be situational or circumstantial would be that of resuscitating a patient in the car park. This may mean that infection, prevention and control policies are bypassed and the right equipment may not be there, or there is no time to wait for the right equipment. Some actions may be clearly contra to the 'rules' but the circumstances create the behaviour.

In fact, intentional violations of rules and procedures occur every day – these are called workarounds. These workarounds can then become normalised behaviour; that is, the constant change in behaviour becomes the routine.

This is behaviour developed over time, often without the workforce's knowledge. Much can be learned by understanding why violations happen, and why certain violations become the norm. It may be that the rules or procedures no longer apply or are causing risks or unsafe care so people are rightly working around them. The key issue is to ensure that learning from incidents outweighs judgement and the deterrent effect of punishment, and that staff feel able to speak out, raise concerns and challenge rules and policies that may put their patients and colleagues at risk.

Negligent conduct

Negligence is conduct subjectively more culpable than human error or risky behaviour but could be either. In fact negligence is not behaviour; it is a legal term that arises from both civil and criminal liability systems. If this is found by law to be the case, the person or organisation that is negligent must pay for the resulting damages. In the UK this is stated as: the healthcare system owed a duty of care to the patient or patients and the healthcare system breached that duty of care and the patient or patients were harmed by the breach of duty of care. There needs to be a direct link (causation) between the breach and the harm suffered.

Reckless behaviour

This is where someone makes a behavioural choice to consciously disregard a substantial and unjustifiable risk. A person acts recklessly if they consciously disregard a substantial risk and importantly they are aware of the consequences of their actions. Recklessness is definitely something that should be sanctioned and may even need to be dealt with as a crime – demonstrating in law greater intent than mere negligent conduct; all reckless behaviour therefore should be disciplined. Reckless behaviour may relate to a lack of capability (unable to practise at acceptable standards) or conduct (unwilling to practise at acceptable standards), best summed up as an employee 'who can't do' (capability) or 'won't do' (conduct). The public rightly expects that individuals personally and directly accountable for the delivery of such care will be held to account by both the organisation and their regulatory bodies.

Reckless behaviour can be by commission (doing something wrong) or omission (not doing something right). Acts of omission include professional conduct where individuals failed to act; they may have stood by and witnessed poor care and done nothing about it. This could be for multiple reasons; for example, where at all levels staff felt constrained by the system or others to speak up for fear of the consequences. They may have lacked the courage to articulate the unintended consequences of competing interests or priorities, and by doing so potentially put patient lives at risk.

JUST CULTURE AND DISCIPLINE

We need to understand that the majority of individuals do not intend the error or its undesirable outcome even though the consequences are potentially life threatening.

The team needs to design the system so that it is resilient, so that we pick up the minor things going wrong before they become more significant and so that a single human error cannot lead directly to a catastrophic result. But we judge people in all sorts of different ways, depending upon the outcome of the incident or error. Outcome bias or judgement occurs when the same behaviour produces more ethical condemnation when it happens to produce a bad rather than good outcome, even if the outcome is determined by chance. For example, if a nurse makes an error that causes no harm we consider the nurse to be lucky.

In a good safety culture if the error leads to significant harm the consequence for the nurse should be the same, and the cause of the error investigated to ensure learning. The worse outcome in this scenario is if other nurses witness punitive responses to errors, future errors will go unreported for fear of consequences, which ultimately leads to less safe environments for patients. Staff are unlikely to report incidents if they believe that they are going to place themselves or their colleagues at risk of being disciplined or punished.

An environment which understands the principles of a just culture will therefore help ensure the ability of staff to speak up and where relevant report incidents, from which lessons can be learned and patient safety improved.

To create a just culture we need to dispel two key myths.

- The perfection myth: if people try hard enough, they will not make any errors.
- The punishment myth: if we punish people when they make errors, they will make fewer of them; that remedial and disciplinary action will lead to improvement by channelling or increasing motivation.

A just culture requires that local NHS human resource and disciplinary policies clearly describe how organisations will manage staff involved in incidents, complaints and claims to ensure that they are not detrimental to improving patient safety.

In order to help healthcare managers determine a fair and consistent course of action towards staff involved in a patient safety incident, the National Patient Safety Agency (NPSA) developed the Incident Decision Tree (IDT) based on a model developed by a world-leading academic in the field of understanding error, Professor James Reason. It prompts the user with a series of questions to help them take a systematic, transparent and fair approach to decision making. The IDT helps managers to decide whether it is necessary to suspend staff from duty following a patient safety incident and to explore alternatives, such as temporary relocation or modification of duties. It comprises a flowchart with accompanying guidelines. It does not provide firm answers or decisions, but rather flags a range of possible solutions and/or additional factors to be explored (Reason, 1997).

The Reason model has been adapted in the United States and implemented across a number of hospitals there. It has been modified to apply the following questions.

1. Did the employee intend to cause harm?
2. Did the employee come to work drunk or impaired?
3. Did the employee knowingly and unreasonably increase risk?
4. Would another similarly trained and skilled employee in the same situation act in a similar manner (Reason substitution test)?

If the answers to the first three questions are no and to question 4 is yes, this points to the error being a system problem. The error would require a full root cause analysis to understand and then seek to rectify the system error.

The NPSA algorithm (Reason, 1997) provides an excellent tool to be used as a framework to inform decisions on whether to take disciplinary action and has the potential to drive a more consistent approach among NHS organisations. However, one limitation with the tool is that it does not include a section at the end of the flowchart to determine the action a member of staff took at the point of incident and whether learning from the incident has been realised. The worst case scenario is a situation

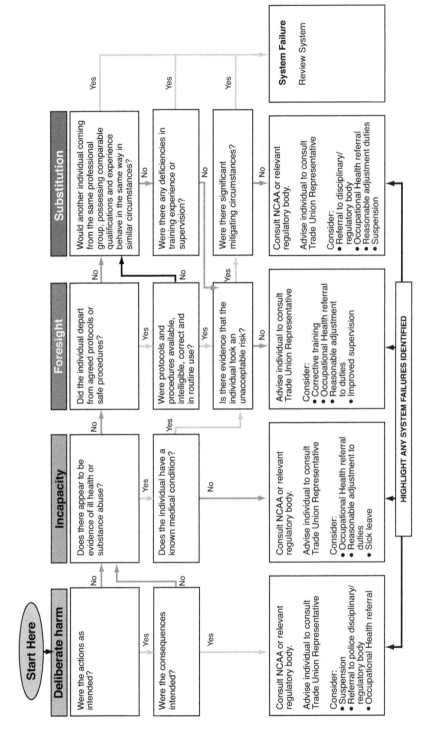

FIGURE 3.1 James Reason decision tree

where a staff member had covered up their mistake, altered records and shows no remorse for the incident that has occurred. In the majority of incidents, in particular where significant harm has resulted, staff can be seriously affected and require support.

JUST CULTURE AND ACCOUNTABILITY

A just culture does not mean an absence of accountability. It is essential in a public service that our actions are explained and that responsibility is accepted. Along with increased public awareness of patient safety issues, there is increasing public interest in the performance of the health service and therefore an increased expectation around accountability.

The many different forms of accountability influence the decisions healthcare staff make on a daily basis, including when a patient safety incident occurs. Accountability for patient safety means being open with patients, explaining the actions taken and providing assurance that lessons will be learned. NHS organisations need to demonstrate the right balance between both accountability and openness.

There is a wide range of literature available via sites such as The Health Foundation, Health Improvement Scotland, and in the United States the Agency for Healthcare Research and Quality (AHRQ) and the Institute for Healthcare Improvement, which underpins the emerging thinking about developing safer systems for healthcare; there are also strong economic and business arguments for improving safety and reducing harm in the NHS. There are a number of actions the organisations can take to assess how their trust is doing in terms of reducing harm and promoting a safety culture. These include the following.

- Review their current disciplinary policy to ensure that when incidents are investigated there is an understanding of human factors and the just culture. The key issue is to ensure that learning from the events outweighs the deterrent effect of punishment and staff feel able to speak out, raise concerns and report incidents.

- Conduct a culture survey of their staff and ask them if mistakes are made whether they feel safe to come forward so that the organisation can learn from the event, then feed back the information on a unit by unit basis.
- Review their incident reporting system; if incident reports are mainly about problems with processes and equipment you have a low reporting culture, and in fact these are mainly operational issues that should be reported using a different strategy. If the reports show individuals reporting on other individuals, there may still be a low reporting culture; it is easy to point the finger at others.
- If individuals are freely reporting their own mistakes, they feel they can speak out and this points to a good reporting culture. When individuals act almost against their own self-interest, and report so that others can learn, you know you have a good safety culture. Where individuals report their own violations, they will know that they have a good just culture and that the organisation they work in understands violations are not disciplinary actions and are to be learned from.
- However, the systems approach does not mean that individual actions are put to one side and not considered when reviewing an incident. There is a fine balance between individual actions and system failures that result in an incident either occurring or having the potential to occur. This balance is different for every case; in some incidents individual actions or human error contribute to a much larger extent than systems factors, whereas in other incidents this could be the opposite.

Effective error management therefore requires an understanding of the varieties of human error and the conditions likely to promote them. If human error factors (such as dispensing the wrong dose of a prescribed drug) are identified, organisations and teams can start to find solutions that predict or prevent them and make changes that maximise performance rather than set people up to fail.

An important factor in any safety system is awareness by individuals, teams and organisations of their own levels of safety. With regard to organisations, this is often identified during the annual risk assessment process, and the risk register is the evidence of how safe an organisation is and what measures that organisation is taking to reduce its levels of risk. Staff delivering the care, however, can feel that they have little opportunity to influence the organisational levels of risk or change the system within which they work. A simple tool for individuals and teams to understand their own safety levels has been devised by Professor James Reason (NPSA, 2008).

Professor Reason's model is called the three buckets model. This self-review tool asks each individual (it could also apply to teams) to give themselves a score in relation to three factors: self, context and task. They score themselves; for example, 1 for low risk, 2 for medium or 3 for high risk. The three factors are taken into account in the following ways.

- **Self:** how are they feeling that day; are they preoccupied; are they inexperienced or do they lack knowledge; are there physical factors such as fatigue; are emotional factors and life events affecting their day?
- **Context:** what is the environment, both physical and cultural, in which they will be working; what are the expected distractions, skill mix, team factors, number of interruptions, number of changes or handovers, levels of authority, hierarchy and team interactions?
- **Task:** what are the procedures and activities they will be undertaking during the day; what are their levels of experience, resources, equipment, knowledge and complacency; are there any specific issues in relation to individual patients, such as complexity and vulnerability?

The most important aspect is that staff feel safe to report their concerns, regardless of the level of harm that occurred, to give the earliest opportunity to rectify or reduce further harm and ensure learning has led to prevention of harm occurring to others. Where a culture of blame is in place, leading to a culture of fear, including fear of reporting incidents, the higher is the likelihood these will be covered up and not reported. This is the worst case scenario for safety cultures, and it is important to recognise. Low level reporting of serious incidents suggests that organisations are likely to have significant safety issues that are not being disclosed and subsequently the opportunity for learning has been lost.

Organisations should also ensure that staff receive feedback and are informed of what action has been taken as a result of an incident being reported. Staff are more likely to foster an open attitude if they feel they have been listened to and that by reporting an incident they have made a positive difference to patient safety.

CONCLUSION

Having a just culture encourages a working environment where many factors are taken into consideration and recognised as contributing to an incident, or to the events leading up to it. Research around patient safety has highlighted that the majority of staff try to create a safe environment and prevent things from going wrong. Despite some high-profile cases, the overwhelming majority of incidents are not caused by malicious intent or even lack of competence on the part of the individual delivering the care.

Patient safety incidents should be reviewed to consider events far beyond the actions of the individual healthcare staff directly involved. While human error may immediately precede an incident, in a technically and socially complex system such as healthcare, there are usually entrenched systemic factors at work. The move away from focusing blame solely on individuals, and looking at what was wrong with the system in which the individuals were working, is called the systems approach.

CHAPTER 4

The problem with nursing and medicine

THE PROBLEM WITH NURSING

Nursing has faced a barrage of criticism over the last few years, with many commentators suggesting today's nurses are uncaring, overeducated and lacking in compassion. This is illustrated in multiple examples given in the Health Care Commission Mid Staffordshire Hospital Report of poor care, neglect and uncaring attitudes.

The Francis report (2013) does not provide the answer to the key question as to why nurses came to work at Mid Staffordshire Hospital and provided care of such poor standards, while others kept silent and didn't take any action. The Nursing and Midwifery Council professional code of conduct is very clear about the unacceptability of such practice and yet, despite this, many patients experienced considerable suffering. It appears there was a 'fear culture' and those that did speak up were not supported. However, this does not really begin to explain why so many nurses were involved in continuing to deliver unacceptable nursing practice over this period of time and failed to raise their concerns. Many other professionals, too, would have been involved with the patients nursed on the wards in question, such as medical staff, physiotherapists, dieticians, hospital chaplains, and pharmacists, all of whom are accountable to professional bodies. The questions need to be asked of all staff that were there.

The question of why nurses would come to work to give poor care needs to be carefully explored together with understanding the context in which they work. It is too easy to seek simplistic explanations for problems faced by the profession. It is only by looking for the origins of the problems that we can start to understand what has happened and do something about it.

HISTORY

Nursing has changed considerably over the last few decades. The traditional apprentice scheme of state registered nurse (SRN) and state enrolled nurse (SEN) trained over 3 years was changed to the Project 2000 course, which moved nurse training from a certificate entry to that of a Higher Education Diploma, educated in the university and no longer as paid workers in hospitals. The need to equip the nurse for the future needs of the patients was recognised together with the need to continue to attract those of high calibre into the profession. The enrolled nurse training was discontinued at this time, recognising that the career prospects for enrolled nurses and access to conversion courses was limited. Concerns were raised at the time about the implications, as the removal meant a significant percentage of the workforce was no longer going to be available. The loss of this labour was never truly calculated, and the staffing levels on wards were more often based upon historic patterns than scientifically evidenced matching ratios of registered nurses to the needs of the patients.

During this time the needs of the patients changed significantly. In the 1970s patients undergoing surgery such as hernia repair or appendicectomy had up to a 7-day stay, which meant that wards had a higher proportion of self-caring patients and less dependent patients. Advances in medicine have seen the introduction of day surgery, laparoscopic procedures, and advances in community care (e.g. intravenous (IV) therapy and intensive care at home). In addition demand management schemes advancing management of long-term conditions has led to the patient admitted to hospitals being highly dependent, requiring high levels of not just nursing care but interventions such as cannulation, IV therapy, venepuncture, electrocardiograms (ECG) and the like, once the domain of the medical profession but now passed without additional resources to be delivered by the nursing profession. As the pressure of European Working Time Directives (EWTD) arrived, nurses took on more of the doctors' roles. Commentators in the 1980s warned about the stretching of the nursing profession at both ends; they saw nurses taking on extended roles but not relinquishing any of their existing ones, all without evidence-based calculation of the workforce requirements to ensure quality of care maintained. The emergence of the healthcare assistant (traditionally the nursing auxiliary) roles began to develop during the 1990s, some taking National Vocational Qualifications (NVQs) training to extend their roles, but concerns were emerging around the regulation of the healthcare support worker/healthcare assistant, and the variations of practice that existed between health settings.

BRING BACK MATRON

One statement commonly heard is that 'if only we could go back to the old days of matrons running hospitals then all would be well'. What is missing from much of the debate is, first, an acknowledgment that all was not necessarily well under the old system; there are examples of tyrant style management, and leading staff through fear and by rote were not necessarily conducive to delivering highly sensitive patient-centred care. Second, accepting these myths as reality denies the opportunity to explore a comprehensive diagnosis of the root of the real problem.

There is, however, merit in considering what the perception of 'matron' really means to people. It is the desire to see strong leadership of the hospital which is visible, listened to and acknowledged by all. There is a well-known saying that if Florence Nightingale was walking around the hospitals today she would not be able to find out who was in charge. There is sadly a lot of truth in this as hospitals have become very complex and complicated institutions, with a myriad of structure and layers of confused accountability.

Ward sisters/charge nurses (known as ward managers) today have at least two roles, one is the 24/7 responsibility for the care of their patients, and the other is that management can be for over 50 staff including rota management, appraisals, education, training and supervision of staff, the ward budget, the stock, supplies, management of complaints, incidents, medicine management, supporting relatives, coordination of junior doctors and social workers, and complex discharges to name but a few. In addition to this the acuity/dependency needs of the patients on most wards is high, with at times up to 80% of the patients requiring total nursing care, and on some wards the majority of patients may need help with essential needs such as feeding. The entering of electronic data also adds to this workload, and it is not surprising that today's ward managers are struggling to meet all of the demands made upon them.

Departmental matrons experience similar types of conflicting demands upon them, many spending more time 'counting beds' to deal with bed pressures caused from patient flow through the hospital than providing the nursing leadership and supervision to their ward managers. These matrons (or unit managers) frequently have two line managers, one links to the director of operations, whose priority is more often achieving access targets, and financial balance, and the director of nursing role whose focus is maintaining professional standards, and assuring safety and quality of the patients.

In turn both these directors report to the chief executive, who together with the whole executive team has responsibility for achieving all of the hospital objectives, which include access targets, financial balance, and safety and quality standards.

The chief executive reports to the chair of the board who has the governance role for the organisation. The chief executive is also answerable to the commissioners (clinical commissioning groups – CCGs) who are purchasing their service, and the commissioning authority who monitors their performance, who is in turn answerable upwards to the Department of Health. The arrangements from April 2013 have changed the upwards reporting of the chief executive to the accountable officers of the clinical commissioning groups and the provision of specialised services the responsibility of the National Commissioning board (now known as NHS England).

There is a view that suggests that leaders who are directly accountable for a service should always have full authority over those responsible for the delivery at the front line. Directors of nursing are professionally accountable for the standard of nursing care in their organisation but frequently they do not line manage those staff that are responsible. The line between professional and operational accountability can be a grey one and is frequently misunderstood by the public. The public expect the director of nursing to be 'in charge' of the nurses and don't understand why this is not the case. The role of director of operations/chief operating officer and director of nursing can lead to confusion of accountability, and create difficulties for the ward manager and matrons to be clear where their priorities lie, particularly if the core objectives for the trust are not clearly owned, shared and articulated. Conflicts occur where more nursing staff are required to ensure quality care delivery and cost savings have to be made. It is essential that the director of nursing's voice is heard when there is a need to make savings and close wards.

Debates about whether the director of nursing should have operational responsibility tend to lean towards the view that when finance and day to day targets are priorities, the professional leadership for nursing would always take second place. Supporters of this view would say that the director of nursing role is to provide a counter challenge at the board so that all perspectives can be heard.

It can take considerable courage for a director of nursing to provide the professional leadership required when, for example, they need to effectively challenge decisions to cut nursing posts, as the individual may experience considerable resistance and direct hostility. The key to this is to ensure that the issue becomes the entire board's agenda and they are all fully conversant of the potential risks.

If the culture of the organisation or those assessing the issue is one of blame rather than accountability, it is easy to point the finger at an individual such as the director of nursing or a group of nurses on the ward as responsible for the failings. If the culture is one of a learning organisation, the systems and context of how these failings have occurred need to be addressed effectively. The solution to dealing with such complexities lies with effective leadership and shared objectives and priorities jointly owned by the top team. Mutual respect and shared vision are the key to addressing these difficulties.

STAFFING LEVELS

In some areas the ratio of qualified registered nurses to healthcare assistants and the numbers of nurses to patients have been determined; for example, intensive care units, midwives to births ratios, and more recently stroke units in London. However, in other areas such as 'care of the elderly' we can see staffing levels at their worst. Elderly care and medical wards include the most vulnerable patients, with complex needs and being at high risk from falls and pressure ulcers, and yet the staffing levels for these wards are far lower than those seen in clinical areas such as the elective surgical wards. A number of initiatives have been taken to address this, such as Royal College of Nursing (RCN) guidance and staffing acuity tools (Fenton, 2007), but while the tools were in the main well received, achieving the appropriate funding to match what is required presents a number of problems within the financial constraints of the hospital.

Respondents to a Nursing Standard survey (RCN, 2012) conducted as part of its Care Campaign, identified inadequate staffing levels as the number one reason nurses are struggling to provide high-quality care. Almost one in five of the 2,554 UK nurses who responded said having more staff would improve care quality.

The Department of Health (DoH) has resisted the arguments for minimum nurse staffing levels for many years, the rationale being that organisations will tend to resort to the minimum rather than strive for the maximum. However, in countries where minimum staffing levels are determined and in some cases in statute (e.g. Australia) stories of poor nursing care are rare. In the United States studies have shown improving the ratio of registered nurses to patients reduced mortality and morbidity (Spetz *et al.*, 2009). This work is further supported by the Twigg *et al.* (2011) report on staffing levels in relation to patient outcomes.

Workforce planning in general for nursing has been at best chaotic over the last few decades. There has been a boom or bust approach, with either too many student nurses being trained and not being able to get jobs, or a shortage of nurses which has led to widespread overseas recruitment to try to fill significant gaps. It is possible that when there are severe shortages of nurses that the bar for recruiting top calibre nurses may be lowered, and some evidence of this has been seen where there have been questions of a lower level of competence in some applicants.

Blame has often been aimed at the higher education providers (Carter, 2011) for not producing nurses of an acceptable competence. Changes to curriculum have been made over the last few years, but 50% of the course takes place in clinical practice, with responsibility for teaching in the clinical setting, expert mentoring and assessment lying with the providers of placements. The availability of good mentorship requires sufficient staffing levels and good role models, which are all too often impacted by insufficient staffing levels, to allow the release of nurses for training as mentors, or provide the right learning environment to get the best out of a clinical placement.

ARE THE WRONG PEOPLE COMING INTO NURSING?

A popular myth is that nursing is attracting the wrong type of person, and that today's nurses lack compassion and a caring attitude. Some feel that nursing is no longer considered a 'calling' as in the past. It is true that a very different type of student nurse has emerged over the last few years; they are more likely to be older than the average university student, with an average age of 26 plus, and some will have families of their own. More recently selection processes are specifically undertaking assessments for the 'right attitude' and values, although evidence is lacking that student nurses in general have less compassion than other health professionals such as doctors and allied health professionals (Willis Commission, 2012).

ARE THEY OVER-EDUCATED AND MORE INTERESTED IN GETTING A DEGREE THAN BEING A NURSE?

The arguments for a degree-based profession have been well made and are based upon attracting high-calibre students who have the intellectual and practical abilities to undertake the complexities of nursing in all its elements. Tomorrow's nurses will be expected to hold even higher level critical thinking skills, be able to diagnose, prescribe and treat patients, and care, with high acuity, for an ever increasing group of patients with complex needs. The view that nurses with degrees lack practical skills is not supported in the literature and is not something that would be voiced about other healthcare professionals. Currently England is an international outlier in not having 100% graduate nurses, and it is essential that nursing is seen as an attractive career for students to undertake as a university choice.

GENERATION Y VERSUS THE GOOD OLD DAYS

The world of social networking and texting is producing a very different generation to that of a few decades ago. Students spend far less time in face to face interaction, and focus on other media to communicate. This generation is encouraged to be challenging, questioning and to stand up for their rights, which produces a very different type of student from that which entered nursing a few decades ago.

Student nurses in the past delivered care by practical routine and rigid rules and sometimes in fear of their seniors. While many harp back to the old days and wish for the return of matron, others can recall a 'not so rosy' picture where individualised care was not the norm, and not all was always done in the best interests of the patients.

TOO MUCH PAPER WORK

The amount of not just paper work but overall administration is very heavy for most nurses, and the advent of electronic records appears to have added work rather than reduced it. All nurses are expected to be computer literate and some are running duplicate systems even within an organisation where the software is not compatible, making the goal of service-level reporting and management difficult to achieve. Most ward managers very much value the role of the ward clerk; unfortunately the provision of these posts is not consistent even within one hospital and not necessarily geared to give support for a 24/7 service provision.

The productive ward series (NHS Institute, 2006) recognised the competing demands on ward managers and was specifically designed to 'release time to care' and increase the percentage of time nurses spent in delivering direct patient care. Examples of the series include improvements to the environment (a decluttering and more organised stocks and systems), improvements to meal times, medication rounds, and also some really useful modules for effective leaders. The productive leadership series includes email management and meeting management, both of which are very valuable. When the productive series was first introduced it attracted pump-primed funding and the take-up was very high, but unfortunately as the resource reduced so has the implementation, not only of the productive series but of many other initiatives, of which we are very poor at formally evaluating in terms of their impact.

Sadly, at a time when the NHS needs investment in improvement and innovation the NHS Institute no longer exists. It is essential that access to such expertise and resources is not lost at a time when it is most needed.

REGULATION

There has been considerable debate as to whether healthcare assistants should be regulated. One of the emerging themes to concern both the nursing profession and the public is the amount of direct care delivery that is undertaken by non-registered professionals. The problem with a percentage of nursing care being delivered by staff who are not regulated is there is no way of stopping them from practising where there have been serious failings of care, other than hoping that all future employers are vigilant in obtaining accurate references. The case for regulation is strong, and now further supported by Francis (2013); however, the practicalities of implementing it are fraught with difficulties. First, defining what is and is not a healthcare assistant is problematic, as there are such variations of practice. The National Vocational Qualifications programmes were expected to lessen this anomaly, with the belief that someone with an NVQ level three would be able to undertake a number of delegated nursing functions under the supervision of the registered nurse. Without a regulatory framework there is nothing to prevent any healthcare assistant doing this, and in many cases where access to NVQ courses are limited, healthcare assistants of any level could take on specific roles delegated to them. In addition some healthcare assistant roles include social care, and there are wide variations of practice both across the health service and social care.

The history of nursing in the UK teaches us that this situation is not new, as following the Second World War many nursing assistants took on additional extended roles, which led to the development of the Enrolled Nurse programme. This was a 2-year course, with agreed educational standards, provided by the 'schools of nursing' and leading to admission to the regulated nursing register as a second level nurse. Many of the problems that arose with the enrolled nurse concept were primarily linked to lack of career progression, lack of access to conversion courses and being inconsistently valued in the hospitals; that is, 'in charge of the ward today, but not good enough for tomorrow's shift'. These could be addressed effectively by designing a career pathway that supports rather than restricts progression.

Designing and adequately resourcing a formal programme for health-care assistants leading to registration could provide a solution to the current largely unregulated workforce.

In the current model of regulation the UK has separate bodies for different professions. There have been a number of issues with regulation over the last few years, and the Nursing & Midwifery Council (NMC) has been criticised for the considerable delays that exist for professional code of conduct hearings. There have also been leadership issues and more recently there are plans to increase the annual registration fees which have met considerable resistance. Whether the current model of regulation is sustainable is debatable. In Australia the various professions have been merged into a single organisation, the Australian Health Practitioner Regulation Agency (AHPRA). The registration process is strict, nurses have to demonstrate education points equal to hours of training; for example. registered nurses must show evidence of a minimum of 20 hours' professional development. Admission to the register requires formal written validation by each employer of all posts held in the previous 5 years. AHPRA has registration for both registered nurses and enrolled nurses which they have retained. This is just one example which demonstrates the possibilities of being more creative about registration.

EDUCATION, TRAINING AND RESEARCH

Changes in the funding of nursing education over the last few decades has led to loss of targeted funding for nurses and to significant variation of access particularly for post-registration funding. Formalising the requirements for nursing linked to registration would help to drive standards of care. The Post Registration Education and Practice (PREP) system that was developed by the United Kingdom Central Council for Nurses (UKCC) was expected to achieve this, but lost momentum and did not deliver its original aims. Revalidation has been introduced for nursing with the aim of protecting the patient and ensuring quality delivery, but the funding allocated is far less than that given to medicine, despite the fact that nursing has a much larger workforce.

The need for nurses to be involved in research continues to be important, but it appears that there has been less attention given to research over the last few years. Research and education must be at the forefront of a nursing strategy otherwise we risk continuing to not grow and learn, and ensure the highest evidence-based practice, both in terms of clinical care and leadership theory.

THE PROBLEM WITH MEDICAL LEADERSHIP
Different perceptions of medicine and nursing

It is interesting to note that media coverage denigrating doctors as opposed to nurses is not very common. There have been a few very high-profile cases such as the Shipman and Bristol inquiries, but generally it would appear the public continues to hold doctors in high regard. The contribution that doctors may have had in relation to hospital failings such as at Maidstone Tunbridge Wells and Mid Staffordshire Hospital have not been particularly highlighted despite the links to high levels of patient mortality.

Unlike nurses, the public doesn't appear to criticise doctors for being 'too clever to care' and to lack compassion simply because they have undertaken a degree programme. This observation was highlighted in a recent report commissioned by the RCN (Willis Commission, 2012). Similarly there do not seem to be the debates about whether there needs to be medical leadership presence on health boards. The Health and Social Care Act 2012, which saw considerable controversy, drew particular attention in its early stages to the term of GP commissioning, which was later changed to clinical commissioning after some considerable lobbying by other professional groups. Despite this change, there has still been considerable reluctance to mandate the requirement of senior nurses' appointments on CCG boards.

Medicine continues to dominate clinical research, attracts protected funding for education and training and is able to successfully lobby with the support of the various royal colleges for increases in doctors' posts.

These are just a few examples of the level of power that medicine holds, yet many consultants in acute hospitals would say the opposite, that often they feel powerless, are dictated to by management targets, are working longer and longer hours, with little reward or acknowledgement. Many trusts struggle to attract consultants to leadership positions and there is a general feeling of 'them and us' between doctors and management.

Juniors and European Working Time Directives (EWTD)

In the past junior doctors did the majority of their learning 'on the job' while they worked long hours and gained significant experience. While the experience gained was seen to be beneficial, the long working hours and potential impact on patients from tired overworked doctors led to the adoption of EWTD regulations which restricted the number of hours the junior doctors can work without a break. Those that oppose the regulations argue that this restriction has impacted negatively on the doctors' experience and their ability to acquire the necessary competencies required for senior appointments. Today's junior doctors work a shift system, which can often lead to a lack of continuity with the care of patients and can also impact on their learning.

Junior doctors, like nursing students (although the latter are likely to be slightly younger), are also part of a generation that has grown up with social media, leading to a reduced exposure to face to face communication. Similar to students of other professions they are usually more questioning and challenging, articulate about their rights, and at the same time are starting their careers with large student debt, less job security and the potential reduction of high-level pensions at the end of their career.

Most junior doctors will complain about the amount of administration and paperwork they have to contend with. Some trusts have developed physician assistants to support juniors with simple clinical tasks such as cannulation, venepuncture, and some have looked at providing administrative support to allow more focus on the clinical aspects of the role.

The changes to junior doctor training and reduction in working hours does not leave much space for leadership development. There have been some recent attempts at programmes for specialist registrar (Spr) level, and a number of bespoke leadership programmes. There is some evidence that where specialist registrars take postgraduate managerial qualifications and buddying arrangements with managers the results are productive (King's Fund, 2011). If we are going to equip the future medical workforce to deliver high-quality care there is much more to be done. The British Association of Medical Managers (BAMM) (now discontinued) was an organisation that used to support medical leaders, as did the work of the NHS Institute.

Consultant career for life

The current system appoints consultants to organisations with the mutual expectation that this is a job for life. As the consultant settles into the role they usually incorporate a level of private practice which is supported by their credibility as an NHS consultant.

During their career the consultant will undergo annual appraisals, but these will often tend to be more clinically focused and separate to the organisational objectives or job-planning process. Feedback from errors, complaints and general benchmarked performance may be limited and often only brought to attention if they choose to or there are significant concerns. The revalidation process has begun to address this.

The reality of the 'job for life' consultant is that many of them believe they have 'seen it all'; they have watched management teams and chief executives come and go. A minority will positively engage with leadership opportunities and become clinical directors and work with innovative executive teams, while others may become cynical after a period of time and return to their full-time 'job for life' post.

Job planning/consultant contract

Historically hospital consultants had a contract that differs considerably from that of most NHS hospital employees' traditional 37.5-hour week.

They are contracted to undertake sessions of programmed activities (PAs) allocated to their clinical work, such as theatre, outpatients and so on. Most have a contract for around 10 PAs a week, including a small number of PAs for supported activity such as administration, teaching, professional development and research. There are also additional PAs to cover on-call requirements.

Currently the consultants' work programme is negotiated annually via a process called job planning that aims to align the consultants' work to the needs of the patients and to reflect changes in services and organisational needs. In reality this process lacks consistency both within organisations and across England.

To date there is little formalised performance management of consultants. The use of data to compare productivity, error rates, complication rates and patient feedback is improving when used to support appraisal and subsequent revalidation but mostly it is limited to the revalidation process rather than linked to employment with the trust. The current levers to achieve change and address variations in practice are difficult to achieve, and attempts to introduce such measures are commonly met with significant resistance. Some of this resistance would be seen to be quite reasonable, as a large percentage of consultants work very hard, undertake long hours and demonstrate considerable commitment to their patients. It could, however, be argued that this commitment is being delivered more at an individual level and the process usually fails to collectively address productivity improvements such as improved turnaround times for diagnostics, admission avoidance and reduced length of stay.

Balance of private and NHS work

Many medical consultants in England enjoy some level of private practice, this being fitted around their NHS contract and their individual job plan, and this tends to establish them within the locality in which they both live and work. In the majority of cases consultants will remain in the same role for many years, as moving away from their 'job for life' post would most likely result in the loss of their private practice income.

There are a couple of recent threats to the future of NHS consultant private practice. First, many hospitals are undergoing acquisitions, mergers and service reconfigurations. In some cases these changes require consultants to move to other hospital sites and/or work between multiple sites. The second threat is the fast emerging private sector as real competition to the NHS, examples of which include outsourcing of diagnostics and elective procedures, which is having the impact of driving down the costs and reductions in private income. The future of private practice will most likely see a reduction in private fees as competition and new technology start to impact and private companies look for the best value for money, rather than simply appointing their local NHS consultants to provide the care.

Clinical leadership

Doctors spend large amounts of the health resource on areas such as drugs, surgical innovations and using the clinical judgements and professionalism to justify expenditure on the basis of their perceptions of best practice and evidence-based medicine. Hence the tendency for government to exert some controls (e.g. NICE guidelines, consultant contract, General Medical Services contract, patient choice, NHS tariffs and the like), to apply some consistency in and restrictions on expensive practices. The majority of hospitals have structures which include a number of clinical specialty directorates headed up by a clinical director, who more usually will be a medical consultant with some years of experience, with the aim of providing clinical leadership to the specialty area and supported by a general manager or service manager type of post. The philosophy is one of being clinically led and managerially supported; however, there are a number of tensions that tend to develop with these arrangements. The time allocated to these roles is usually in the form of supported activities within the job plan, and these can vary hugely between organisations, some having up to 2 days to undertake the role and others as little as one session. The experience of being a clinical director tends to see them become rapidly overwhelmed by the number of meetings, email burden, large amounts of management jargon, and the dominance of the need for finance savings and the achievement of hospital targets. Their original hopes of leading improvements in quality of care, and their influence on resource allocation, are often not realised in the way they had anticipated. In addition to this the training for these roles is often limited, and not all feel they have been adequately prepared and supported for this role. Some may also experience hostility from their clinical colleagues, and they may experience conflicts where they may be required to address the poor performance of a difficult colleague.

Medical directors

In a similar way to the director of nursing, the medical director has accountability for the medical care of their organisation but not necessarily the authority or the direct line accountability. In medicine as with nursing the line between professional and operational accountability can be thin. The preparation for this role is usually gained through the clinical director route, but medical directors have a high need for the support of the consultant body. While the post is not one specifically of election, there appears to be an unwritten rule of this requirement. The majority of medical directors in acute hospitals are selected by management from within the organisation and continue to undertake clinical sessions alongside their colleagues. This can make the implementation of unpopular policies, such as changes to job plans or new ways of working, difficult to achieve.

A good partnership and working relationship between the medical director and the director of nursing is essential in providing the professional leadership to the organisation. Their role at the board is to ensure the focus of the organisation is high-quality care delivery. Their job is to make sure the board is fully conversant, engaged and aware of data/facts related to the quality issues in the organisation and that they are fully briefed of any potential risks that may be evident. The combination of strong medical and nursing leadership can be very powerful in promoting high-quality care; conversely where this combination is not apparent, there is the potential for this to not be the case.

General practitioners and CCGs

The transfer of power between primary care and secondary care has been the focus of government policy over the last few decades. The 2012 Health and Social Care Act placed the GPs in the driving seat for commissioning healthcare and proposed that they work in clinical commissioning groups. An important aspect of this role includes governance and monitoring the quality of services delivered. In a similar way to medical consultants, GPs' exposure to leadership roles has been mixed. Some have undertaken roles on professional executive committees, some as chairs within primary care trusts. Many report similar frustrations to those of clinical directors, the wish to provide clinical leadership and be supported by managers rather than dictated to by them. The same issues of undertaking clinical leadership roles in addition to clinical commitments exists, as do the conflicts with the balancing of organisational objectives and retaining the support of GP colleagues.

The Health and Social Care Act 2012 gave the GPs a huge opportunity to take up a leadership role, and they are being held accountable by the National Commissioning Board (NCB, subsequently known as NHS England) for the quality of their commissioning and have the direct responsibility for this. This could prove to be the greatest opportunity for really achieving clinically led commissioning, although whether they are ready and adequately equipped for this role remains to be seen. The act created considerable controversy and Nick Timmins (2012) posed the question of whether in time the health minister (Secretary of State for Health), Andrew Lansley, responsible for introducing this act will be seen as the minister that destroyed the NHS or conversely turned out to be its saviour.

The importance of effective, visible senior clinical leadership has never been so important, and public commentators will no doubt continue to state that the current level of demand for healthcare is unsustainable. The King's Fund (2011) investigation into the 'the sort of leaders the NHS needs' concluded that one of the defining weaknesses of the NHS over the last few decades has been the lack of involvement of clinicians, specifically doctors, who have by far the highest influence on how health resources are used.

The evidence of the relationship between medical engagement and optimum financial and clinical performing is growing (King's Fund, 2011). The attendees at the IHI conference held in Auckland in 2012 included a high percentage of medical consultants and lead GPs, who have taken the lead in parts of New Zealand in driving safety and quality. Berwick's (2012) keynote address at the conference highlighted the critical role medical leaders have in their influence over the use of the health resource. His belief is that engaging these medical leaders in determining the most effective use of this resource is crucial. He described the current level of waste in healthcare and the need to focus on prevention of harm, and reduction in the use of unnecessary tests and procedures that were believed to be causing more harm than benefit. He gave examples of how some of the royal colleges had come together to specifically address the issue of overuse of diagnostics. Doctors have probably the greatest influence on variations in patient outcomes, and Taitz *et al.* (2001, citing King's Fund, 2011) agree, in that not only should the clinical leadership of doctors be at the centre of the management of health organisation, but the absence of this can lead to very poor outcome for patients, particularly where there is dysfunctional leadership and low medical engagement. Bohmer (2012) provides some useful tools in the testing of medical engagement within an organisation and collating some of the learning from IHI.

The work of IHI (Reinertsen *et al.*, 2007, citing Bohmer, 2012) highlighted the number of organisations that don't have a specific strategy on actively engaging its lead clinicians. They provide a useful six-phase framework, which includes: discovering common purpose; reframing values and beliefs (i.e. patients being partners in their care); agreeing a plan; supporting the implementation of the plan; showing courage (up to the board level); and adopting a leadership style that supports engagement. Bisognano (2012) in her keynote speech at the IHI conference described the need for a social movement which moves away from 'what's the matter medicine' to a patient-centred approach of 'what matters to me medicine'. The NHS Institute and the NHS Leadership Academy (Bohmer, 2012) define medical engagement as doctors who will consistently say positive things about their organisation, intend to stay and practise in the organisation and strive to achieve above and beyond what is expected in their daily role.

The parallels between leaders of successful organisations and the findings from IHI and the NHS Institute are very consistent, and the evidence is powerful of the need to urgently engage the medical leaders of the profession to improve the quality of care delivery. Both organisations offered a number of useful tools and checklists to help organisations engage their potential medical leaders.

CHAPTER 5

Soundings from a sample of top leaders in health

This chapter includes soundings from a sample of top healthcare leaders. The aim is to explore their views on the qualities which led them to their top jobs/roles relating to healthcare, and also what they thought some of the features of top performing health organisations were in the UK. It was particularly interesting to hear their views on what they thought good leadership looked like, and what they observed when this leadership was poor.

The importance of including these detailed narratives in this book is to draw out their views and experiences and look at how combining their accounts with some of the theories of health leadership could help in determining where the most appropriate improvements to leadership could be best targeted.

A number of top leaders were contacted and asked if they would be willing to contribute to the book; the majority agreed. These are in effect simply an 'opportunistic' sample, many of whom the author has had the pleasure to work with over the last few years. They don't claim to be representative of top leaders in any particular way, but the very nature of their successful careers suggests they have something that is worth learning from. They comprise a number of participants who have very strong track records, which have led them to have held very senior and influential positions over many years. The group of senior health leaders includes executives, non-executives, medical, nursing, education, public and private sector leaders, the aim being to give a balanced view from across the spectrum of healthcare leadership.

All were given a questionnaire to complete (*see* Appendix 1) to state their views on what they believed to be the key components of successful organisational leadership, where they felt there may be significant issues to be addressed and their views about what action could be taken to make the improvements necessary. The respondents were also offered a follow-up interview to explore some of the issues they raised in more depth. During the interviews they were all incredibly candid and very willing to share their unique insights into what they feel needs to be done to address many of the current difficulties facing the leadership of the health service at this time.

Capturing the views of this group was essential to achieving the aims of this book, as their wide range of very senior leadership experience helps to bring the leadership and management academic theories to life. This was a real opportunity to gain a rare insight into what they think needs to be done to address the current problems facing the leadership of healthcare. It was very important the views and experiences of these highly successful leaders were captured and recorded to not only support the aims of this book but also to share these insights for those aspiring to be top leaders in the future.

The following pages include their responses in full. Further discussion of their responses is given in Chapter 6.

The Rt Hon Lord Philip Hunt PC OBE
Former Chairman, Heart of England NHS Foundation Trust and Member of the House of Lords

Philip Hunt is a member of the House of Lords and Deputy Leader of the Opposition. He speaks for the Opposition on Health, Cabinet Office and Lords reform. He chaired the Heart of England NHS Foundation Trust from 2011 to 2014. He is President of the Royal Society of Public Health. He was appointed as Life Peer in July 1997. He served for 10 years in the 1997–2010 Labour Government. He resigned in 2003 over the Iraq War and returned at the 2005 general election.

He was Deputy Leader of the House of Lords and Minister of State at the Department of Energy and Climate Change from 2008 to 2010. He also served as a Minister in the Department of Health, Department of Work and Pensions, Department of Environment, Food and Rural Affairs and the Ministry of Justice.

He was the first Chief Executive of the NHS Confederation, and previously Director of the National Association of Health Authorities and Trusts (NAHAT) from its formation in 1990. He ran its predecessor organisation, the National Association of Health Authorities (NAHA), from 1984 until 1990. He also served as a member of the Council of the International Hospital Federation from 1986 to 1991. He was President of the Family Planning Association 1997–98 and co-chaired the Association for Public Health from 1994 to 1998.

Lord Hunt attributes his successful career to his ability to be able to articulate a vision and focus on the key issues. He believes he has a high level of resilience and the ability to build trust with staff and stakeholders. He thinks some of the key features in the leadership of top performing health organisations include having a clear idea of what needs to be achieved and the ability to communicate to everyone in the organisation and beyond.

Lord Hunt feels very strongly that organisations must have leaders who have high integrity and who are absolutely committed to safety and quality. His experience suggests that while all trusts would aspire to this, a key requisite in a leader who really does mean it is the ability to listen, who promotes an open culture, and where people feel able to express and escalate concerns. He believes that while there are undoubted efficiencies to be got out of the system, the current Cost Improvement Programmes (CIPs) are virtually impossible to achieve without impacting on quality of care, particularly if patient–staff ratios are unduly affected.

Lord Hunt believes some of the key problems of organisations with challenging performance issues include a failure to understand the organisation and its people, a lack of vision, and inconsistency and poor leadership.

Lord Hunt notes a particular characteristic of weak leadership is an inability to cope with strong but legitimate challenge within the organisation. Chairmen and non-executives can play an important role here. Most have a pretty good idea of their executives' strengths and weaknesses, and have a 'smell for the truth'. He also believes that the 'company/board secretary' has an essential role in raising concerns directly with the chairman. He feels these are very important jobs, 'but the right people don't grow on trees'.

Lord Hunt considers that most non-executives go through a robust appointment process, but they often have limited time to undertake the role, and as they can't be around all the time they need to focus their activity. This often centres on the board meetings and its subcommittees. But, an important aspect of a chairman's role is to encourage the board to meet frontline staff, and to take part in safety visits to the clinical areas where they can hear staff concerns at first hand.

Lord Hunt believes the ideal characteristics of a top leadership team include a shared vision which is communicated to everyone within the organisation with absolute honesty and integrity. Resilience is essential, with the ability to deal with whatever is thrown at you.

He feels we should recognise in the pay of senior executives the huge responsibilities they carry and is very concerned that the average time chief executives remain in post is often short and does not create the long-term stability required to deal with very difficult challenges.

The NHS continues to waste huge amounts of money on pay-offs to senior executives and yet we don't invest sufficiently to support them in their difficult roles. Succession planning for chief executives is poor, and national leadership is required. He says if we were to think of the NHS as a huge company, such as NHS PLC, we would have a consistent approach to selection processes, and development programmes. He felt that the NHS was fortunate to have so many leaders of high calibre and commitment. The challenge was to use them as effectively as possible.

Dame Ruth Carnall DBE
Former Chief Executive, NHS London Strategic Health Authority

Dame Ruth Carnall DBE was appointed as Chief Executive of NHS London in April 2007. Prior to that, from 2004, Ruth worked as a freelance consultant in NHS London and government departments including the Prime Minister's Delivery Unit and the Home Office. Ruth was a non-executive director at the Cabinet Office until 2010 and until April 2007 was a non-executive director at Care UK PLC and Chair of Verita, a small private company that undertakes investigations and enquiries in the public sector.

Prior to 2004 Ruth worked in the NHS for over 25 years. During this time, she undertook senior leadership positions at local, regional and national levels. Her career began in finance, holding various posts in a number of NHS organisations before taking the position of finance director at Hastings Health Authority in 1987. In 1992 Ruth became Chief Executive at Hastings and Rother NHS Trust. She was Chief Executive of the West Kent Health Authority for 6 years before she moved to the civil service to take the position of Regional Director, South East and then Director of Health & Social Care for the South. From April 2003 until the end of September 2004 Ruth served as Director of the Departmental Change Programme at the Department of Health.

Ruth is married with two grown-up sons. She was awarded a CBE for services to the NHS in 2004 and received a DBE in 2011.

Ruth attributes the success in her career to her clear vision and ability to articulate and persuade others. She feels she has empathy and an ability to understand another's point of view but without necessarily sympathising. She also has a willingness to make tough choices and decisions when these are needed.

Ruth believes some of the key features in top performing health organisations include the need for the leadership to show vision, energy, commitment, communication skills, visibility and engagement. She also feels it is important to show occasional bravery but to do this with a lack of ego.

One example of this includes the implementation of one of the much needed service changes which have challenged London over the last few years. Medical leader Lord Ara Darzi headed up a large-scale clinically led strategic project 'Healthcare for London' that proposed radical change in the way acute hospitals were configured across the city. One component of this was the reconfiguration of stroke services, which included designating a smaller number of hospitals as 'hyper acute stroke services'. These changes met considerable resistance from the public, politicians and some clinicians, but an evaluation of the outcomes has demonstrated significant improvements in patient mortality and morbidity.

Ruth feels the features of poorly performing organisations include 'behind closed doors working, silo mentality, avoidance of conflict, bullying, ego driven leaders, and poor team culture'. Examples of this have been seen where there have been investigations into serious incidents such as waiting list scandals and the Department of Health's approach to change and reconfiguration of services.

Ruth believes some of the ideal characteristics for a top leadership team include openness, transparency, mutual respect, tolerance, complementary strengths and weaknesses across the whole team.

She feels that the percentage of health organisations that have highly effective top team leadership is only around 20%, leaving 80% where improvements are needed. She believes the reason that some leaders fail to impact on making improvements relates to the increasing complexity that they find themselves dealing with. Some leaders lack the necessary intellectual capability or have had a lack of personal exposure including the political aspects of the role. Some lack self-awareness and the necessary communication and engagement skills required for these complex roles.

When selecting individuals to senior leadership positions she would advocate testing for evidence of vision and self-awareness, also evidence of 'going through the mill' and still being human. She would look for a demonstration of their understanding of what they need around them to succeed, and examples of where they may have failed but learnt from the experience. Ruth feels we should stop relying on verbal and numeric reasoning and use other methods such as observation, case study and role play.

Ruth believes improvements need to be made in making relationship building more permanent. She feels there should be more use of 360 degree feedback processes and these should be a more formal part of appraisal and reward. She feels strongly that organisations should not tolerate or reward bad behaviour. Ruth also advocates the use of multi-day assessments of organisations, which include an in-depth process of reviewing an organisation. Currently, the health authority has had responsibility for conducting these types of reviews.

Ruth would support a framework/tool based on assessing leadership characteristics in terms of selection of top leaders and ongoing monitoring of leadership effectiveness, with an expectation that it builds upon the top leader's programmes we have currently.

Dr Roger Greene
Director, Tricordant

Roger came into the NHS as a graduate management trainee in 1980, having studied for his PhD in Leeds. He spent 26 years in the NHS, 12 of which were as a Trust Chief Executive in two trusts in the South East of England. He left the NHS to start a career in consultancy and became a Director of Tricordant Ltd in 2009. In between the NHS and becoming a Director of Tricordant he spent 3 years as Chief Executive of a Christian charity. He therefore brings a unique perspective to leadership, having occupied top leadership positions in the public, private and voluntary sectors over 20 years.

Roger attributes his successful career in the NHS to his deeply held set of personal values and their fit with the purpose of healthcare delivery (these include compassion, care, integrity, courtesy and humanity). He also has extensive experience and understanding of the 'business', political and organisational aspects of health and care. He values highly the ability to listen and communicate respectfully with people at all levels of an organisation, and to value their contributions.

Roger feels the key features of successful leadership in top performing health organisations include the need to have a constant focus on doing the right things in all aspects of the organisations' dealings. He believes it is important to have a consistent message and ensure continuity of the message. Connection, approachability and visibility are essential and top teams must demonstrate a commitment to the quality of healthcare delivery. He says that if they do this, financial viability and high-quality performance will follow. He also feels that successful leaders demonstrate self-awareness and a constant drive for improvement.

Roger is now one of four co-owners and directors of Tricordant, a consultancy specialising in whole-systems development work across all sectors of public service, commerce, industry and the third sector. They work extensively across health and social care, particularly with commissioners in developing partnership strategy and integrated commissioning arrangements between the NHS and local government.

Both in his previous role as chief executive and in his current consulting role he feels strongly that when he undertakes site visits, in particular speaking to frontline staff, he can very quickly get 'a feel for the organisation'. Similarly he draws on his experience as a patient in several hospitals in the NHS. He describes using the terms of both 'light and dark' organisations, where he senses the 'spirit of the place' by the way in which staff speak about their patients or clients, and how they interact both with him and each other. He looks for staff who are 'attentive', by which he means that if he walks onto a ward someone will attend to him, listen, engage and answer his questions regardless of his status. Conversely there are times when he has felt 'ignored' by staff, who are 'too busy' and his assessment is that if staff are not able to give their attention to him this may be the same experience for the patients and relatives of this area. He observes facial expressions: 'Are the staff smiling or scowling?', 'Is the place ordered or chaotic?', 'Is the member of staff giving me their attention or is their mind on something else and I'm just in the way?' – all of which give a message about the leadership at many levels of the organisations.

Roger feels features of poorly performing organisations include a narrow leadership focus on finance and meeting targets rather than delivering quality care. Frequently the leadership is detached from the reality of the everyday experience of their staff and patients. There may also be poor strategic decision making if decisions have no basis in evidence and the leadership is not aligned with both the internal and external realities of their context and challenges. In his NHS career, he cites observing several neighbouring trust mergers leading to long-term damage to local healthcare provision because they were driven less by clinical and patient care requirements and more by financial and political expedience. He recalls predicting at the time these would end up as 'train crashes' as changes were imposed on colleague chief executives who appeared to have little choice in agreeing to their implementation. He states that some of these organisations are now 15 years down the line and are still in serious difficulty. Frequently past mergers of hospitals led to the significant 'running down' and downsizing of one hospital in favour of the other, leading to a loss of identity, confusion and often a deterioration of services on both sides without a coherent service strategy shaped by patient needs and clinical opinion. He supports reconfigurations led by patient need and clinical quality, but feels very strongly that service change needs to be owned and accepted by the participant organisations and staff, and not simply imposed on them without proper engagement. He does believe that significant changes to health and care delivery are essential for long-term sustainability in the UK, but should be evidence-based and not simply driven by opinion.

Roger believes the ideal characteristics for a top leadership team include unity of purpose and acceptance by all of their corporate responsibility as well as excelling in their professional roles. High-quality medical and nursing directors, for example, should not only champion great patient care, but also champion financial sustainability and good corporate governance. High-quality directors of finance understand the importance of high-quality care as well as financial balance and health. He believes trusting relationships between the teams to be essential, as is sharing corporate goals and ambition, as well as the need for a good balance of continuity and change in the team, 'not all growing old together'. While holding strongly to a collective core purpose, the team also needs a sense of detachment and objectivity to be able to challenge constantly the standards delivered by their own organisations.

Roger gives what he describes as a solely subjective estimate ('a gut feeling') of the current percentage of organisations with highly effective leadership to be around 25% but cautions that there is a lack of facts and measurable evidence to support the view.

Roger believes many of the failures of chief executives are directly attributable to their failure to align their organisation to its own core purpose. In the case of hospitals the core purpose is the delivery of high-quality healthcare and treatment. He commented that it is not uncommon in the UK for chief executives to be 'parachuted' into struggling organisations to 'turn around the financial problems'. All too often this is achieved at the expense of quality and leads to an organisation which is not sustainable for the future as it has not embedded high-quality care as its core purpose.

Roger's view is that communication of the core purpose to all staff is essential and they need clarity from the top of the organisation that quality matters. He cites an example of arriving as the newly appointed chief executive in his second trust to discover that staff at many levels of the organisation believed that commissioners had told the previous management of the trust that they were only paid to 'treat patients and not to care for them'. Whether or not this was a myth or a careless slip of the tongue by a healthcare commissioner, the point was that many of the staff had swallowed the message that they were not 'paid to care' and felt genuinely dispirited by the message. He and the leadership team set about correcting that view by engaging the staff in developing a new sense of mission, vision and purpose that quite explicitly built in the purpose of caring.

Roger commented in his interview that the bookshelves of the world are groaning under the weight of 'what you need to know about leadership stuff' but with relatively little research and evaluation to know what genuinely works. The research findings of Jim Collins and his associates in *Good to Great* (2001) and *Great by Choice* (Collins & Hansen, 2011) are now highly influential in his thinking, as is a seminal article entitled 'In praise of the incomplete leader' (Ancona *et al.*, 2007). The latter expounds the theory that it is not possible for 'one leader to be all things to all people' – if they try they will invariably crash, burn out and fail. On the contrary, it is the norm for leaders to be 'incomplete' and self-awareness of their weaknesses is essential for there to be a balance of skills in any leadership team to both build on strengths and offset weaknesses.

Expanding this theme, Roger describes the work Tricordant have undertaken in developing the concept of their 'distributed' leadership model to create a whole and healthily balanced leadership team across the four key dimensions of identity, strategy, systems and culture.

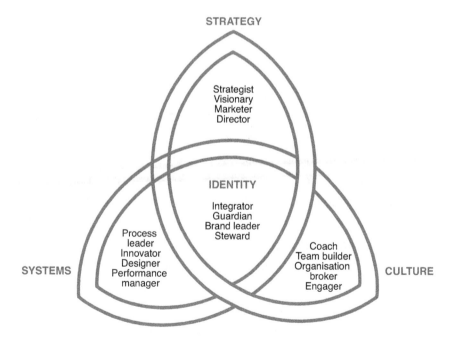

FIGURE 5.1 The Tricordant leadership model

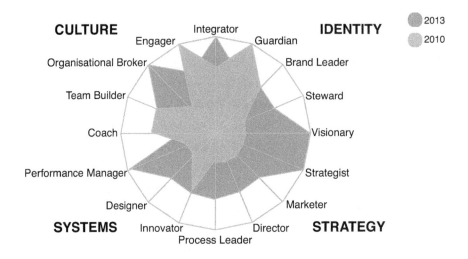

FIGURE 5.2 Tricordant leadership model diagnostics

Tricordant have developed the model to offer a suite of diagnostic and development tools that can build distributed leadership into the fabric of an organisation and remove reliance on the heroic and charismatic model that is so often reliant on individuals and the art of 'making the right appointment'. One aspect of the diagnostic is illustrated above, comparing a leadership team in 2010 to its ambition for 2013 (*see* Figure 5.2).

Roger believes this model can be used by boards, including non-executives and chairmen, to help recruit to executive posts by undertaking a diagnosis of the balance of skills in the existing teams and identifying where the gaps are. This can influence strongly the selection and recruitment of leaders who are committed to an organisation's core purpose and identity. It can also help develop the potential in team members through valuing the importance of the various roles they play, as well as identifying and helping resolve potential conflicts.

Regarding governance, Roger believes the way in which trust boards are configured and voting rights distributed can influence heavily the quality of delivery of healthcare. He gives the example of estates or information management and technology (IMT) directors, who are frequently responsible for critical systems aspects of care. For example, if the IT infrastructure is not in place, clinicians are unable to function and spend valuable clinical time doing 'paperwork', often duplicated in several areas, or when the estate does not support the delivery of a quality clean environment to care for the patients. Often these directors have a minimal voice at the trust board, whereas the responsibilities they carry are mission critical in the delivery of quality care.

Dr Anne Rainsberry
Regional Director, NHS England (London Region)

Dr Anne Rainsberry was appointed as the NHS Commissioning Board (now known as NHS England) Regional Director for London in June 2012. Anne joined the NHS Commissioning Board from NHS London where she was Deputy Chief Executive and an executive member of the board for 6 years. Anne has worked in the NHS for 27 years. During this time she has undertaken senior leadership roles at local, regional and national levels. Anne has operated at board level since 1995, working in acute and community organisations. She joined the Department of Health in 2001 as Director of Development for the South East Regional Office and then moving to lead this agenda across the South of England. In 2004 she became a member of the Department of Health's management board leading on the delivery of the department-wide change programme. In 2006 Anne returned to the NHS to take up a board-level role with NHS London and in addition to these responsibilities from 2010 has been the PCT Cluster Chief Executive for eight PCTs in North West London where she has led one of the largest service reconfigurations across the NHS and developed a major integrated care scheme covering over a million people.

Anne attributes her success to having a clear vision of what needs to be achieved. She also feels it important to build good teams around her to ensure delivery of the vision. Anne also believes it essential to create the necessary energy and resilience to ensure sustainability.

Anne asserts that the key features of successful leaders of health organisations include transparency, supportive challenge and creating the ambition to deliver the best. She gives the example of the implementation of the stroke strategy for London. The implementation of this change was successfully led and carried out amid intense opposition from a number of stakeholders. Evaluation of this change has shown significant improvements in both mortality and morbidity for stroke patients across London. The success of the implementation is that the vision was led by clinicians and they were able to demonstrate that by focusing services on a smaller number of specialist stroke units outcomes could be significantly improved.

In contrast Anne sees the key features of poorly performing organisations as being closed cultures, which do not welcome or embrace enquiry or challenge and instead focus on the wrong things such as targets, rather than placing quality at the centre of their core purpose. The key example of this is the Mid Staffordshire Hospital, where focus on the finance and targets were pursued at the expense of safety and quality care delivery.

Anne believes the ideal characteristics for a top leadership team to include being passionate about quality care, having the ability to engage people and to be able to work across boundaries.

When asked what she believes to be the percentage of health organisations that have highly effective top team leadership she makes a guess of around 50%. Anne believes the reason that some leaders fail to impact on making improvements to direct care delivery is because they focus on the wrong things and don't create the environment for others to drive improvement. They also don't empower clinical leaders. In terms of what needs to be done to improve both the selection and ongoing monitoring of top leadership teams in relation specifically to their impact on quality and safety delivery to the front line Anne feels that commissioners should hold top teams more directly to account. Anne also believes that chief executives should be selected as much for what they have done to improve care as they are for financial achievements.

When appointing to top leadership positions Anne would look for evidence of their vision and passion for improving care, their ability to inspire and energise others and their ability to navigate the system and remove obstacles to improvement. Anne proposes that in addition to standard selection process they should also include evidence of case studies, group exercises, and increasing face to face time during the selection process.

In terms of ongoing monitoring of top team leadership effectiveness Anne proposes more thorough board development and challenge and formal annual feedback from the National Trust Development Agency or through Monitor for foundation trusts.

Sue Bernhauser OBE

Non-executive Director, East Sussex Healthcare NHS Trust (a combined acute and community trust)

Sue Bernhauser, MBA, BSc Nursing, RNT, RCNT, RGN, RNMS, was previously Emerita Dean of Human and Health Sciences, at the University of Huddersfield. In 2013 she was awarded an OBE for services to nursing and healthcare in the Queen's Birthday Honours.

Sue has held numerous roles in practice both in general nursing and learning disability nursing. In 1981 she completed a Certificate in Education, and she has been Head of Nursing, Midwifery and Health Visiting, Deputy Dean of the Faculty of Health, University of Brighton (14 years) and Dean of Human and Health Sciences, University of Huddersfield (7 years).

She has also held a number of non-remunerated positions which include: member of the Board of Governors, University of Brighton; Executive Committee Member and Chair of the Council of Deans of Health; involvement in committees at the ENB/UKCC/Nursing and Midwifery Council; Member of the Prime Minister's Commission advising on the Future of Nursing and Midwifery in England; Member of the Calderdale and Huddersfield NHS Foundation Trust (CHFT) Partnership Board; Member of the Nominations Committee, and Calderdale & Huddersfield Foundation Trust Member of the Chief Nursing Officer Advisory Committee (England).

Sue attributes her success to having a passionate commitment to the 'business' she is in, her excellent communication skills which include successful networking, and recognising that a great team is more effective than individuals within it.

Sue believes some of the important features in the leadership of top performing health organisations include being clear and articulate and understanding the business you are in. She also feels successful leaders demonstrate high levels of visibility, and achieve this by 'walking the floor'. These successful leaders have a strategy of inclusiveness and engagement with people. Sue cites as examples of this chief executives she has worked with who staff in the organisation know; these are individuals with well-developed communication skills who 'talk to anyone'.

An example of where Sue has seen effective leadership was in a local trust she worked with when she was Dean at the neighbouring university. The features present were a committed, stable top team, with executive members who had been in post for some years. The chief executive here was committed to the NHS values, continually striving for improvements, and prepared to forgive, learn and not blame where mistakes were made.

Sue feels where leadership fails is where there is a lack of managed communication and a sense of the people at the top being 'distant'. Where this is the case employees are unsure of what the organisational priorities are, and how they 'fit in'. Sue recalls having worked in an organisation where the staff really did not know any of the executive team and this leads to staff believing that there is a lack of organisational cohesion at the top.

Sue believes leaders such as the nursing director and finance director need to be visible in terms of working together, such as visiting care delivery areas, and there needs to be demonstrable respect between colleagues and an understanding of respective 'functions'. She also feels that professional credibility is essential.

Commenting on the Mid Staffordshire inquiry, she gives the example of how important it is to meet patients' most basic needs; for example, her own worst nightmare would be having to wait to go to the toilet, so her own practice would always be to make sure that never happened to patients in her care. Sue believes that once staff start to cut corners and lower standards it becomes easier to do it again and then the behaviour becomes normalised, in that staff fail to notice. She also feels that patients are generally very forgiving if for example their pain relief is a bit late, but are very concerned about the way people speak to them and how they are made to feel. Sue feels strongly that in cases where poor nursing care is identified the process of consequences for nurses found guilty of breach of professional standards needs to be very clear.

Sue feels staffing levels are an issue and where they fall below safe levels then care will inevitably be affected. She fully supports the need for agreement of minimum staffing levels, and also she feels nurses need to be better educated in prioritising care. She believes the leadership (ward sister/charge nurse) should view the ward as a whole and work with staff to prioritise the most important aspects of care. She believes that nurses are very good at prioritising the right things to do in emergencies such as cardiac arrests, and the same type of discipline should be applied to all care.

She estimates the percentage of health organisations with effective top team leadership to be around 30% and believes the reasons that some leaders fail to impact on making improvements to direct care delivery include a lack of communication and interpersonal skills, being 'in it for the money' and having 'no passion' for what they do. These leaders tend to lack understanding of the business at all levels. Sue talks of the general tolerance of 'mediocracy' within healthcare leadership, and the view that 'so long as no one is doing harm, things are okay'. She also believes that many are 'promoted beyond their competence' and a lack of career planning has led to some leaders unsuitable for such positions finding themselves in these roles without the necessary skills. Effective honest career planning she believes would help some individuals to remain in the roles they are most effective in rather than be promoted to those they don't have the skills to do.

In terms of directors of nursing, she is encouraged and feels that the calibre has improved overall. She also feels that the nursing voice is being heard more at the board these days, and by contrast cites a trust she knew of a few years ago whose board reports in a 3-year period had no mention at all of nursing.

Sue feels that partnership working between higher education and the trusts is essential and that she wouldn't hesitate to inform the director of nursing if there were concerns being reported by student nurses about the care in the organisation. Relationships are important along with trust between organisations to make sure issues are highlighted and acted on. Sue cites the work she did on the Prime Minister's Commission into Nursing with the previous government on the value of service and education working as partners.

Sue believes people selected for top team roles need to demonstrate evidence of previous success and high levels of personal and professional credibility. When appointing to top leadership positions she would look for evidence of excellent communication skills, a track record and evidence of success and the potential to 'grow' into the role. She states she is 'not a psychometric test person', but she does advocate some form of pre-selection including some kind of 360 degree 'reference'. She also proposes all candidates do 2 weeks in the organisation (while accepting this may be difficult to achieve), and proposes the use of personal 'case studies' of successful activity, which have been validated. Sue also reiterates the need for more effective career planning, and talent spotting of junior nurses and doctors with the potential to become effective leaders for the future.

In terms of ongoing monitoring of top team leadership effectiveness Sue suggests success of shared objectives between contributors, and peer evaluation from a similar institution's top team. She also feels that it is important to ensure that the induction of non-executives is done well. Sue adds that she considers ongoing monitoring is more important, as selection has been 'done to death'.

Sue is unclear whether the NHS Leadership Academy will help to address some of the health leadership problems. She supports the work the King's Fund has done with developing leaders and providing a network and group of peers that can support each other. In terms of addressing culture she thinks the academy will need to think more creatively about how this can be achieved effectively.

She concludes that any tool that helps to assess areas for development and improvement is long overdue.

Professor Elizabeth Robb OBE
Chief Executive, Florence Nightingale Foundation UK

Elizabeth Robb is a registered nurse and midwife, holds an MA in Nursing and is a registered midwifery teacher. She is a Visiting Professor of Leadership and Nursing Practice at London South Bank University.

She was Director of Nursing and Clinical Governance and Deputy CEO at East Somerset NHS Trust for 12 years. She was then appointed Director of Nursing at North West London Hospitals NHS Trust, where she was subsequently also made Director of Infection Prevention and Control and Deputy CEO. She is a former Florence Nightingale Foundation Leadership Scholar and was appointed Chief Executive of the Foundation in April 2010.

In 2009 she was awarded an Honorary Doctorate by The University of West London in recognition of her research on reducing avoidable hospital mortality. In April 2010 she was also appointed as a Non-executive Director of NHS Professionals Ltd.

Liz in her current role as Chief Executive of the Florence Nightingale Foundation has successfully taken the foundation to a new level. She is a highly respected nursing leader in the UK, and has unique skills not only in the leadership and influencing of nursing, but in her wide networking, seeing the benefit of working outside of nursing with wider professionals, partners and stakeholders to ensure nursing is not considered in isolation but as an integral equal player in the leadership of healthcare.

Liz attributes her success in her senior roles to her ability to create a compelling vision of the future and engage clinical staff at all levels, along with her ability to understand the difference between assurance and reassurance and her ability to turn data into meaningful information. This has been a very important feature in her board working, as well as being able to demonstrate an understanding of the business, political and financial elements of her roles in organisations, and having a clear patient-centred focus.

Liz believes the key features in the leadership of top performing health organisations in terms of their impact on frontline care delivery is the need for leaders to be able to articulate a compelling vision and be able to engage all clinical professionals. It is essential to have a fair and just culture which encourages openness and transparency and puts quality outcomes and the patient experience at the heart of all they do. She feels strongly the need for leadership from the point of care to the board, and quality goals to be part of every leader's role (explicitly), as well as the importance of leaders being able to understand the difference between assurance and reassurance.

Liz gives the example of when she was a member of a board that subsequently successfully achieved foundation trust status. She attributes this success to the board having an absolutely clear vision of why this was important and spending a huge amount of time getting the staff and general public on board. Excellent communication was the key.

In this and many other of her roles she highlights the success of clinical leadership training and has seen lots of positive impact from the Florence Nightingale scholarships, the matron/senior nurse training where there has been a focus on skills and behaviours, and use of data to empower staff to positively influence and make improvements to the quality of patient care.

Liz believes that where an organisation is 'in turnaround', and has really worked on their culture, for example with improved training and communication with staff as an aspect of their improvement strategy, this has had really good effect.

Liz describes the key leadership features of poorly performing organisations in terms of the impact on the frontline care delivery as those which use command and control cultures to achieve targets and which fail to engage professionals. She has concerns about organisations who 'talk the talk' about quality driving all they do but fail to follow through by embedding it in business and operational processes, job descriptions and the like, and also where there is poor use of data for assurance or improvement.

An example of this is where board reports for complaints/incidents have lots of graphs and data but no intelligent analysis that links possible cause and effect, or have no follow-up actions. Some executive teams say quality is their business but the board only receives performance monitoring within divisions and service units that focus on finance and activity.

Another example is seen in organisations where individuals are failing to report issues, as the impact is seen as blame of the individual, rather than focusing on the systems or processes that may have led to the failure.

Liz believes the ideal characteristics for a top leadership team of a health organisation include the use of data as management information to make decisions. Liz feels the team must have the ability to set a compelling vision for quality improvement and patient-centredness. Good leadership (not just management) skills and ability to use different styles appropriate to the situation are essential as are great communication skills and active listening skills and a focus on staff engagement. She feels that leaders must be seen to be setting standards and 'walking the walk' not just talking the talk.

Director of nursing role

When asked specifically about her views on the director of nursing (DON) role as a member of the top leadership team, Liz states that these individuals need to be courageous and engaged in more than just nursing, be able to challenge constructively when necessary with supporting evidence and bring meaningful reports to the board. It is important to bring care issues to the board; for example, hearing patient stories and the views from frontline staff, to give the board the opportunity to hear and highlight the good, the not so good, and what the real challenges are.

Liz states that DONs need to get out there, which doesn't mean simply doing a 'clinical day' but being known by staff, engaged with the nurses, providing vehicles for staff to meet and exchange ideas, and engaging the front line in the nursing vision.

Liz believes the DON's job is not easy; it means being strategic and constantly focusing on the standards of care. It is much easier to go and 'sort out A&E' when they are having a challenging day, but there is a need to plan and address the longer term issues. Some DONs can lose their focus on the professional issues, their role on the board was always meant to bring the patient perspective and challenge where patient care may be compromised. Often the dynamics of the board make it difficult for the DONs to challenge and it's much easier to keep quiet. Challenging takes courage and can risk alienation and being accused of not being corporate.

Examples of this relate to challenging low nursing numbers, and planned reductions, where there are financial imperatives to reduce cost. It is the DON's role to ensure the board are aware of the risks and that a full impact analysis is done. This is not always well received, and can at times mean the DON may need to take this further, such as going directly to the chair, or writing to the whole board. This is not an easy thing to do, and some of the DONs are not adequately prepared for this role. You need experience to challenge, and some of the newer DONs have not had that exposure, either to board working or to the day to day operational roles as nurse/service managers. Some of the most challenged organisations recruit DONs in their first post who have not had the necessary senior-level confidence built on experience.

The role of the director of operations and the DON's role can, on occasions, cause tensions, as the director of operations' main focus is on achievement of targets and financial balance, whereas the DON's role must be the quality and safety agenda. While this is at times a difficult relationship to manage, Liz would not necessarily recommend combining the two roles, as there could be a risk of the professional issues always taking second place. The key to avoiding tensions is to work on relationships of mutual respect and trust.

Effectiveness of top teams

Liz estimates the percentage of health organisations that have highly effective top team leadership to be around 20%. She believes the reason that some leaders fail to impact on making improvements to direct care delivery are rooted in their failure to address the key elements of culture, leadership, right staff/skills and full engagement.

The features of these types of leaders is they are often in denial that they have problems, even when problems with leadership of the senior team are highlighted. Instead of looking themselves at how they can change and better engage the staff in the organisation, they refuse to hear or acknowledge that they are the problem and so blame other individuals. For example, if the issue is perceived as poor nursing care, they may blame the nursing leadership, rather than taking on joint responsibility and examining the full evidence and context.

There are a few chief executives who are more interested in being popular with the staff. They celebrate their visibility within the organisation, seeing visiting the clinical areas as a demonstration of their impact instead of really engaging and hearing the issues from the front line and agreeing to get more information and plan solutions with the team. They can focus on anecdote and seek to blame without thoroughly investigating the issues.

The concept of 'management by anecdote' is often a feature in failing organisations, and this can lead to the wrong type of solution to resolve the problems, as the full facts do not get established and plans are not made to address the wider root causes.

What can be done

Liz's view is that a number of things could be done to help improve both the selection and ongoing monitoring of top leadership teams, specifically regarding their impact on quality and safety delivery to the front line.

She describes a number of leadership development initiatives in the past, for example the Leading Empowered Organisations (LEO) 3-day course, which offered nursing staff training in leadership as just one example among many. She felt one of the problems with these types of courses is they fire up the ward managers to drive changes, but the organisation doesn't support them when they return from the course. When she was a DON she took the whole board through the same 3-day LEO course, which meant that the top team and the ward sisters were talking the same language and better understood how to make change happen.

She felt there have been many initiatives but not many have been formally evaluated against impact on service improvement. Teams and their leaders should be appraised to include their actual quality improvements.

She also believes there is a need for greater understanding of the culture in organisations and described a concept known as the culture barometer. She described an example of a culture barometer being piloted by a small group. There are a few tools around aimed at testing the organisation on ability to change, and the positive culture for optimal delivery of care.

Liz feels strongly that getting the culture right is one of the keys to successful organisations alongside alignment of strategic and patient care goals. In terms of selection processes for top team positions she feels it is important to ensure the job description is explicit about the role, particularly for the DON; there needs to be absolute clarity about what they are responsible for.

When appointing to top leadership positions the qualities within the individual she would look for are evidence that they demonstrate understanding that their healthcare organisations actually serve the public; an understanding of the meaning of quality improvement; an appreciation that 'culture eats strategy' (that is, culture is at the heart of the organisation); and good quality leadership skills, interpersonal skills, empathy and ability to actively listen.

There is a need to test values at interview and in particular testing the individual's ability to challenge effectively, and part of the selection process should also include role play, such as with a patient complainant, and also exposure to teams of staff on Q&A sessions.

In terms of ongoing monitoring of top team leadership effectiveness

Liz advocated team appraisal based on outcomes achieved; getting feedback from clinicians and patients and regularly appraising the organisation's and local culture.

Liz's view was that a framework or specific tool based on assessing leadership characteristics in terms of selection of top leaders and ongoing monitoring of leadership effectiveness would be very useful.

Dr Peter Carter OBE
Former Chief Executive and General Secretary, Royal College of Nursing (RCN)

Dr Peter Carter OBE previously headed the Royal College of Nursing, the world's largest professional union of nurses. The RCN has a membership of over 400 000 nurses, midwives, health visitors, nursing students, cadets and healthcare assistants. Before assuming the post of RCN General Secretary in January 2007 Dr Carter spent almost 12 years as Chief Executive of the Central and North West London Mental Health NHS Trust, one of the largest mental health trusts in the UK with an international reputation.

Dr Carter is a graduate, and a member, of the Chartered Institute of Personnel. He also has a Master's Degree in Business Administration and a PhD, both from the University of Birmingham. He was awarded the OBE for services to the NHS in the 2006 New Year's Honours. He is a visiting professor at the Florence Nightingale School of Nursing and Midwifery at King's College London and Anglia Ruskin University.

Peter attributes his success in his senior leadership positions to a number of things, including experience and credibility and feels that he has gained a great deal from his past roles. Prior to his role in the London Mental Health NHS Trust he had a Director of Operations role in London and Bedfordshire for 6 years and gained experience chairing the London Mental Health Network for a number of years.

He credits his success to his ability to look at things objectively, and having the skills to take a step back; he believes that far too many leaders are subjective in their decision making. Peter feels strongly one of the most important features is to have the courage to do the right thing, even at times when it's not necessarily the easy option.

He states that good leaders demonstrate clarity of objectives, priorities, and direction, and ensure the organisational architecture supports this. He believes it is essential for leaders to be inclusive of the people (i.e. the staff) and they must have the ability to communicate and relate/translate to frontline staff. This means they must speak the language which brings people on board. He says that it's the provision of this clarity that gives reassurance to the staff and to the various stakeholders.

He believes the key features for leaders of top performing health organisations include having the ability to really understand the clinical agenda, being really tuned into what it is about, and being care orientated. He explains this is about being truly patient centred with quality of patient care being the absolute core business of the organisations.

Peter feels there are many times where there can be tensions between the managerial agenda and the clinical agenda, where sometimes they are seen as being in opposition. He believes strongly that the agenda for healthcare is clinical, and that management cannot be seen to be different. He gives an example from car production: their product and output is their business, and he says you wouldn't see their managers not caring about the quality of the cars being produced; they wouldn't say that's a different job. In healthcare the delivery of quality care is the core business, in the same way you can't separate clinical objectives from management, as they have to be the same.

Peter feels that features of poorly performing organisations where an organisation fails include where the board lacks insight about where things are going wrong, and/or are focusing on the wrong things. There is often a disconnect between the leadership and its organisation.

Peter's view is that trusts meeting their targets doesn't necessarily mean they are a top performing organisation. When he walks around a hospital he gets a feel for the organisation, which is usually based on positive feedback from the staff. However, he has met some ward sisters who don't know who their director of nursing is, let alone the other members of the executive team. He feels strongly that where this is the case, the top team have little engagement with the front line and this ultimately impacts on frontline care. 'Where no one knows the senior executives, where frontline staff, particularly ward sisters, do not know who their director of nursing is, you are in trouble.'

Peter goes on to say he has seen a number of chief executives who say they 'love visiting the wards' as if it is a Sunday outing, and so often this is seen as a rare event rather than a systematic process and an opportunity to really hear and act on what the frontline staff are saying. There are some boards who are genuinely surprised when they hear there is a problem in their organisation, whereas other suppress 'bad news' and work to keep problems away.

Peter believes it is important for top leadership teams to demonstrate a real mixed economy of skills, clarity of role, responsibility, knowing what they are responsible for, and are truly patient centred. These leaders avoid jargon and they connect with staff. So often there is an assumption that frontline staff understand what executives are talking about when it is felt to be 'jargon' and not related to what matters to the frontline staff. Peter feels strongly that successful directors of nursing understand this; they understand the agenda of the front line and they tune in and translate to give meaning.

Peter feels the percentage of health organisations with a highly effective top team leadership is around 80% that are ranging from good to very good, but 20% are struggling which, even though it sounds a small number, still equates to a lot of trusts. Peter backs this up with the findings of recent report on evidence given to the Health Select Committee where Monitor says 11 foundation trusts are in serious financial difficulty (Guardian, 2012).

Peter believes the reason why some leaders fail to impact on making improvements to direct care delivery is they are subsumed in chasing targets and balancing the books at the expense of patient care. He talks about some 'who get by on a wing and prayer, dodging bullets' and believes there is a widespread practice of appointing people who are inexperienced. He feels that some are simply out of their depth, promoted too early, and lack credibility, and consequently the casualty attrition rate is very high.

He gives the example of where he feels there is frequently a classic case of directors of nursing getting on and doing the job, trying to fix the problems but not flagging up formally enough and escalating serious problems. He sees them going on to subsequently lose their jobs. While very occasionally this may be justified, more often the trust finance director has set a financial target, and they coerce and pressurise the director of nursing into making cuts. In the case of directors of nursing, there are often two scenarios.

- The director of nursing (DON) is leant on by the finance director and the chief executive (often both male) so the DON goes ahead and makes the cuts. If, subsequently, serious failings emerge the DON is held responsible because they went ahead, and the impact of the cuts had not been sufficiently flagged up in a formal enough way. Too frequently there is no documented audit trail of a record by the DON expressing reservations on the impact of cuts and the subsequent impact on safety and quality. It is thus the DON's word against others where this is an absence of email records, and minutes where concerns are expressed etc. This frequently leaves the DON isolated and vulnerable.
- The director of nursing does the right thing, writes a paper which includes a formal risk assessment, presents it to the board and highlights the risk of unsafe services. The board then knows the risk. Sometimes this is heard and acknowledged by the board, other times the DON may need to go above the chief executive's head and deal directly with the chairman; this may work or may sometimes may lead to them losing their job.

Peter feels that many directors do not engage their non-executives and chairs enough. 'They do not have the conversation or build relationships.'

Chairs can be supportive, but there are times where they can become insulated from the state of their organisation. There may also be occasions when approaching the chair is blocked by chief executives, who may feel undermined.

Peter believes much could be done to improve both the selection and ongoing monitoring of top leadership teams. He believes we need to effectively prepare people for senior leadership positions, pay more attention for succession planning, which includes giving future leaders exposure to the board and executive working. He feels the development of political skills is essential and the need to learn to use and relate to non-executives and chairs more effectively.

Peter feels strongly these are very senior jobs and there is a need for applicants to be subjected to a high level of analysis. The selection process for executives needs to be far more rigorous, including scrutiny of standard CVs, and also the involvement of outside assessors. He supports the use of assessment centres that really test out why people want the job, using probing questions. It is important to test for integrity, honesty and sensitivity, and find ways in which these can be more effectively assessed.

Peter is concerned about the attrition rates of executives which is very high, chief executives in particular. Within the organisations there need to be far more formalised robust appraisal systems, peer group support and proper mentorship/supervision. He feels there needs to be greater support and use of formal coaching and learning sets. The RCN has set up a confidential networking learning set for DONs, to give them the opportunity in a confidential setting to share issues and explore solutions for particular problems. Peter feels these can be very isolated jobs, and the RCN programme has so far been accessed by a number of senior nurses who are finding the support beneficial. These types of programmes need to be structured and not casual meetings in order to be most effective.

Peter reflects that in the past the regional strategic health authorities had a role of external scrutiny of organisations, particularly in relation to the functioning and performance of the top teams. He feels a concern as to who would do this now, and that the clinical commissioning groups will not have the experience to do it. He believes it is very unclear who will have this important role in the future. 'With so many organisations in difficulty this is a huge worry.'

Baroness Audrey Emerton
Life Peer; President, Florence Nightingale Foundation; Dame British Empire, Dame Grand Cross Order of St John of Jerusalem

Baroness Emerton has had a long and distinguished career in the NHS culminating with her chairmanship of the former Brighton Health Care NHS Trust from 1994 to 2000. She was at the forefront of developing excellence in nursing care in the NHS for many years. She qualified as a State Registered Nurse, State Certified Midwife and Registered Nurse Tutor, and undertook a Senior Management Course at King's Fund London, as well as General Management Course at Administrative Staff College Henley. She has held roles as a Staff Nurse, Ward Sister, Nurse Tutor, Director Nurse Education, Chief Nursing Officer (12 hospitals), and Regional Nursing Officer South East Thames Regional Health Authority.

Baroness Emerton has previously held the roles of Member General Nursing Council, Chairman English National Board for Nursing Midwifery and Health Visiting, Chairman of the United Kingdom Central Council for Nursing, Midwifery and Health Visiting. She has been a lay member of the General Medical Council, Chairman Brighton Health Care NHS Trust, Trustee Kent Community Housing Trust, Trustee Burdett Nursing Trust, Director Defence Medical Welfare Service, Patron Burrswood Christian Hospital/Nursing Home, Chairman National Association Hospital and Community Friends, Member of the House of Lords Science and Technology Select Committee, County Nursing Officer, County Commissioner, Chief Nursing Officer, Chancellor and Chief Commander St John Ambulance The Priory of England and Islands and Deputy Lieutenant Kent. She holds seven honorary degrees/fellowships.

When describing her own leadership qualities Baroness Emerton says she has a number of very strong principles. She states that she never loses sight of the family or patient needs when in a leadership role and ensures that she values the staff of all disciplines and at all levels of any organisation. She believes herself to be a good team player, and uses influence, persuasion and understanding of where people are coming from on which to base decisions. She feels high-performing leaders know how to balance education and experience of practice, are politically aware, and are able to have a wide understanding of context. This includes holding a good knowledge of economics, understanding of both national and international context, together with being knowledgeable about regulatory frameworks and wider strategic plans. Key to successful leadership is a strong culture of quality, where the organisation's values are understood, and that high-quality patient care and safety always comes first.

Baroness Emerton attributes her success to being able to step outside her role, and she gives an example of when she was a regional nurse and the only female on a new team. She describes her enthusiasm and passion with new ideas for improving care and how that wasn't always as well received as she had hoped. She identified a problem in the region of a high incidence of pressure sores/ulcers which she felt was linked to poor quality and inadequate supply of linen that was provided by the supplier of the laundry. She raised this at the weekly meeting with the other executives, and the solution offered was to put her in charge of the laundry. While this was outside her portfolio she agreed to take on this role, and spent time touring laundry sites, meeting with managers and staff who were initially quite hostile to being questioned by the regional nurse. After talking to the staff and explaining to them the importance of the quality of their job of providing sheets without creases or holes to prevent pressure sores, and therefore benefiting patients, they changed their attitude and felt more valued in how they contributed to improvements in patient care.

The second example Baroness Emerton gives is the leadership role she undertook in the closing of two large institutions for patients with learning disabilities and transferring them to be supported to live in the community. This role was given to her and was required to be delivered on top of her day job. She took on the leadership of the task, establishing a project team from scratch, and undertook the challenge of changing many hostile attitudes as to why the change was needed. These included the medical staff who didn't want the institutions to close, parents and carers who didn't want the closure, and the community who didn't want it either. Despite this, the task was achieved over a 10-year period, where every single patient was assessed according to physical, mental and environmental needs, supported by a university department, with the input of high level research and education. She attributed the success of the project to commitment to meeting individual patients' needs, staff training, and the planning of appropriate community services, which ranged from home to community staffed accommodation. She was able to change attitudes through education and training, and through commitment to the values of best care.

Baroness Emerton described similar examples where a hospital implemented protected meals for patients in hospitals. Initially she found that they had set up a working party without including staff from the kitchens or housekeeping. She firmly believes that by involving frontline staff and including the catering staff who are involved in what needs to be changed, success will be far more likely.

Baroness Emerton believes successful top teams set the culture for the organisation: they need to understand their roles and live the values; they need to listen and take action based on the best evidence. Each member of the leadership team must not be afraid to work outside of their given role parameters if they have something to offer that will benefit patient care.

Ideal characteristics of top leaders include openness and transparency, evident at all levels of leadership throughout the organisation. There should be no 'ivory towers' and the leaders need to be visible, walking the floors, and known in the organisation. She says that she has been shocked at the number of directors of nursing who are not known by their ward staff.

Baroness Emerton gives an example of the quality of discharge policies, and how the lack of understanding of patients' needs when they are discharged into the community presents a large problem. She believes effective leaders listen to patients and carers, and know the communities they are linked with, and a good policy is drawn up between organisations to ensure that patients don't fall through the gap in service provision.

Baroness Emerton believes the root causes of poorly performing organisations are directly linked to culture. These organisations are inward looking, closed, and don't place quality at the centre of their business. Examples of this include Mid Staffordshire Hospital, but also many others that have undergone similar levels of enquiry and share the same features, including staff shortages, lack of supervision, and education and training. She has, with five colleagues, been working on the piloting of a 'culture barometer' (which followed on from the Winterbourne View hospital's poor treatment of learning disability patients in 2010). A tool has been developed to test for positive or negative culture, with the aim of taking action to make improvements. She feels strongly that a culture barometer can be used as a reflective tool for all staff including board staff, and to detect if there are areas causing fear and anxiety. This tool can be evidenced by demonstration of the setting of and adherence to the values, and the culture of the top team. This work has now been taken over by NHS England and will shortly be available when guidelines have been published.

When asked to give an estimate of the percentage of health organisations with highly effective leadership she takes a guess at between 20% and 50%.

The reason she believes some organisations fail is that the leaders are inexperienced, and have not had broad enough exposure or worked within a wider context, or outside of their professional specialty. Baroness Emerton describes the benefits of her early management training at Henley Business College, where she was exposed to issues outside of health. She began to read the *Financial Times*, learnt about economics and developed a broader understanding and approach to management and leadership.

Baroness Emerton describes some of the current challenges directors of nursing face; for example, the accountability for care without necessarily the direct line management of the nurses, where directors of operations may have this role. Her solution is not to merge the roles but to have the skills to work around it. She believes that the Chief Nurse/Director of Nursing has a duty to probe, question and challenge and have good understanding of what is happening in the organisation. They must use evidence to influence and direct best care. Baroness Emerton believes that not all have the experience to do this.

In discussing what needs to be done, Baroness Emerton believes succession planning should start much earlier, and talks about how, in the past, nurses needed to undertake formal training and assessment to progress through various roles. Nurses could not become ward sisters, charge nurses or matrons without undergoing each layer of training and preparation for the role. The result of this was that ward sisters/charge nurses had breadth of experience and a discipline of learning.

Baroness Emerton believes that many young people do not know what nursing is about. When she has spoken in schools many don't initially see nursing or midwifery as the career of choice, but once she starts to talk about the profession of nursing many begin to show interest. She also encourages young people to join extra curricular organisations that develop knowledge of life outside of school and build confidence mixing with other people. She built her own self-confidence during school years by joining St John Ambulance as a cadet. She usually finds that there are none of the current student body doing anything similar, but most do show they would interested if it was offered to them.

In terms of how selection to leadership roles could be improved, she speaks with passion about nursing, and how the status of nursing is far too low at the moment. She observes this at all levels, and gives examples of the impact of excluding nurses from key decision-making bodies where they would add value.

She believes strongly that opportunities such as those given with the Florence Nightingale Foundation are highly beneficial in developing leadership scholars, but feels we need to go further with gathering more funds for bespoke leadership training. She cites the very successful Westminster experience programme as one example of political development but feels we need to develop further similar programmes for other aspects of healthcare leadership. Baroness Emerton touches briefly on the NHS Leadership Academy, and while supportive of the concept, feels addressing the issue of organisational values and culture is the absolute priority.

When appointing to leadership positions, Baroness Emerton would look for detailed evidence of previous success in leadership roles; she would want to know what candidates have learned and what they would bring to the job. She emphasises the importance of proven record as opposed to 'talking a good talk'. In relation to nursing she would start with the applicant's values and understanding of culture, and would look for someone who demonstrates wide contextual understanding, and understands the whole patient pathway in how it relates to the multidisciplinary team, both in- and outside the acute setting. She would look for someone who has 'tenacity of purpose' and demonstrates the ability to overcome difficulties.

In terms of monitoring the effectiveness of teams she would start with the culture and look for examples like case studies that demonstrate the values, such as the care of staff, valuing of staff and rewarding and praising staff for high quality, and celebrating success.

Baroness Emerton has huge concerns about the issues of the elderly and believes that much more needs to be done to address the cost of care, particularly in relation to those with dementia. She believes this needs to be tackled at government level, with strong nursing leadership, which includes a roundtable of the various stakeholders such as social services, carers and mental health services. She believes there is a need to focus directly on increasing numbers of nursing staff, and the percentage of registered to nursing assistants, based on evidence not only from the UK but also internationally. She is appreciative of the most recent work completed by the National Institute for Health and Care Excellence (NICE) for staffing levels in acute hospital wards but this leaves many areas without the benefit of the work just completed by NICE, for example the community, mental health and learning difficulties areas all need attention in order that safe, high-quality care can be delivered to the patients' satisfaction. She feels strongly about the need for certification of healthcare assistants and believes this can be achieved. Her concern is that resources need to be found in a time of resource cuts, even though the evidence of benefit from safe levels of staff and cost effective delivery of care is overwhelming. She also believes there is the opportunity to reduce waste of resources, by coordinating care more effectively, supporting more care in the community, and reducing duplication, which will in turn release resources.

Baroness Emerton concludes there needs to be greater attention given to succession planning throughout the professions of nursing and midwifery from the most junior to the most senior roles both within the NHS practice and universities for teaching and research. Succession planning should also be considered by government departments, members of Parliament and Peers in the House of Lords, and the regulatory body the Nursing and Midwifery Council. The profile of nursing and midwifery requires positive publicity and all nurses should be encouraged to promote the profession positively to raise the status of the two professions in the public eye.

Dame Professor Donna Kinnair DBE
Director of Nursing Policy and Practice, Royal College of Nursing

Dame Donna was the Director of Nursing for South East London NHS Cluster and before that her previous posts included Director of Commissioning and Nursing for Health and Social Care in the London Borough of Southwark. Donna worked as an expert nurse on the Prime Minister's Commission on the future of nursing and midwifery in 2010. In 2008 Donna was awarded the DBE for services to nursing. She has a background in law and teaching. Donna believes that good systems and processes can lead to better outcomes for patient care.

Donna attributes her success to her strong 'visionary approach' and her ability to sell 'that vision' to staff. She is very clear about what she wants to achieve and feels she is able to encourage buy-in through allowing staff to formulate the 'how' of what needs to be achieved. It is important to appoint a strong team around her and she is comfortable when others have 'far better ideas' than she does. She believes strongly that visions are usually a collective, in the same way that delivering the vision requires input from many people. Donna feels it is very important to be true to her word by delivering what she says she is going to do; she believes this builds up trust in her as a leader. She also feels that when something can't be achieved then it is important to say so, with a view of what can be achieved. This is because at the outset not every vision is the right way to do something, and changes in direction or approach may be required. Donna also feels that 'courage' is an important quality as it is means that 'you are really committed to tackling whatever you may face in delivering the agenda'.

One example given is where Donna wanted to get a group of consultant paediatricians to set up child protection systems across several boroughs in South London. When she initially approached clinicians they were very rude and extremely angry and distressed about the need to implement new guidance. Donna appreciated that they were vital to the implementation of the new policy as they were also from the range of providers within the boroughs and their involvement was required in order to develop a systematic approach to the protection of children. As she was new to the role, she couldn't work out what she had done to deserve the treatment and so decided to go talk to them all as individuals to find out what as paediatricians and psychiatrists they wanted to achieve and what their concerns were about implementing new guidance. Most of their concerns were that they felt overworked and they were unwilling to entertain implementing anything that required more work. She explored with them as individuals what could alleviate their concerns. She also approached the director for public health of the strategic health authority, whom she knew was well respected, with the suggestion that she host a day for the clinicians. They developed sessions addressing the concerns and explored some of the solutions to them. Together with clinicians she developed an advisory group, which ensured a systematic delivery of child protection systems and processes across the health economy. A real concern for the doctors was the lack of support in court work on child protection issues and writing statements. Donna reassured them she would make herself available to them if they contacted her on receiving any court orders and would support them through the process, as this would skill them up to support others. They, in turn, as an advisory group, met and planned the child protection system and wrote the necessary procedures and protocols. These later became national exemplars.

Another example was where she wanted to improve the care given to families with children with disabilities as a result of learning lessons from a Part 8 review of a child death. None of the clinicians could agree on why there were deficits in services to children with disabilities and each health education and social care agency seemed to blame the other for poor service provision. After several meetings in which the professionals could not agree she asked health visitors to invite families whose children had disabilities, and interacted with all agencies to describe what they needed from the services, and how the services could meet the family's needs in a better way. Donna, alongside the clinicians, mapped the patients' requirements and started to build services to meet these needs. This resulted in taking steps to prevent families and their children having to return to see different professionals, as the professionals came together and where appropriate saw children together. There is now a one stop shop service with clinicians, social workers, teachers and allied health professionals working together.

Donna believes one of the key features of the leadership of top performing health organisations is having staff who have different leadership styles but who are committed to the agenda. She feels that transformational leaders have a place, but it is important to recognise that different leadership styles are appropriate for different occasions and situations. It is also important for good leaders to listen actively to those delivering patient care as often they have already diagnosed difficulties and formulated solutions. Even if they haven't done this, actively listening means that they embark on a joint process of hearing concerns and thinking through what the concerns are and what needs to be done to address problems or needs that service users have. Leaders should be visible, and tapping into the talents of their workforce to try to achieve improvements in clinical care and services is vital. Those who appoint replicas of themselves, who pose no challenge to the system, or those who refuse to appoint those whom they see with the potential to be better than they are do the NHS a disservice as well as those whom we serve.

Donna includes as one of the features of poorly performing organisations dictating without listening, supported by superficial diagnosis, and analysis of perceived problems not based on evidence but on assumptions. It is a mistake to believe that the NHS is a monolithic organisation, as the system is a collection of organisations and there is no one type of fix that can be introduced for the whole system without it being aligned to organisation needs. Another is the concept of 'power' being invested in one person, who mistakenly thinks that their appeal to the workforce using personality or charisma is enough to hold a system together. Other features include a failure to work as a team (with clinical staff) and ensure that the real problems we need to solve have been identified. There is sometimes an emphasis on the adoption of a ready-made solution rather than transparently and honestly dealing with identified problems or issues that our patients bring to our attention. This in turn can lead to a system where, rather than seeking to solve the issues, we just constantly change the leadership.

Examples of poor leadership are many, and most organisations which display it focus on singular fixes, such as financial fixes at the expense of listening to junior staff or patients. Donna cites 'Mid Staffordshire and Bristol' and many of the child protection inquiries as demonstrating a 'just get it done culture' where morale is lowered.

Donna believes that good leaders motivate and inspire the staff by being out there communicating and formulating with staff the vision and mission. Good leaders demonstrate behaviours and values that top teams should hold and show they are worthy to lead. They have good communication (including listening) skills to show improvement and success and when necessary provide encouragement.

Donna feels the reason that some leaders fail to impact on making improvements to direct care delivery is they don't ensure that quality care is the goal and that the financial improvements or efficiencies are a consequence of good care. The focus is too often on an individual target or components of quality such as infection control and we look at these things in isolation without understanding the consequences or impact on total patient care. For example, quality is frequently expressed as the need to achieve the A&E 4-hour target rather than providing care as soon as humanly possible and therefore the result is to plan for maximum timescale rather timely care. Too often staff blindly follow instructions, forgetting the goals even when the outcome proves the direction of travel to be the wrong one.

Donna believes there is need for a combination of competency assessments and testing for those delivering quality health services. She thinks there should be testing of awareness about the components of quality and safety issues. She very much supports the provision of an NHS leadership academy but believes it needs to be proactive in taking the new recruits to support them as top leaders. She believes that objective, independent assessment of top leaders is a must. She wonders if this were to be introduced whether it would result in a more diverse workforce – she cites the success of this approach in selection to medical schools.

When appointing to top leadership positions the qualities Donna would look for include evidence of a person's belief in quality health services, in wanting to make the organisation the best. Also looking for a person who is visionary and able to communicate the vision, able to challenge but humble enough and able to work with a diverse workforce.

Donna supports the use of a framework for selection of top leaders but stresses the need for it to be simple. She feels the selection process needs to include putting individuals through specific scenarios with independent assessors so that situational judgements can be assessed.

In terms of ongoing monitoring of top team leadership she believes there is a need for individuals to self-appraise combined with ongoing audit of leadership qualities and the relationship to delivery of outcomes. She feels there needs to be an objective way of measuring this.

Professor Trish Morris-Thompson
Director, Clinical Quality and Clinical Governance, Barchester Health Care, Former Chief Nurse, NHS London

Trish Morris-Thompson trained at Whipps Cross Hospital in East London, and qualified as a Registered General Nurse in 1982 then as a Registered Midwife in 1986. Trish has a BA (Hons) in Health Studies and Applied Social Sciences (1991), an MBA from Hull University (1993), and in 2007 was awarded a Visiting Professorship by the Faculty of Health and Social Care at London South Bank University. Trish has extensive experience in healthcare gained through her work in London, the East and West Midlands, and South Australia. Prior to taking up her role at NHS London Trish was Executive Director of Nursing for the former North East London Strategic Health Authority. Trish is currently on secondment to the Care Quality Commission.

Trish attributes her success in leadership positions to being inspirational, inclusive and decisive.

Trish contends that the key features of successful leadership teams in healthcare organisations are a culture of staff engagement and involvement, a clear sense of purpose and vision and consistent demonstration of corporate values by the leaders. Trish's view is that where there is evidence of good board leadership and a culture of valuing quality above finance and performance then frontline staff recognise and acknowledge this. Examples include leaders who involve staff in setting the direction of the organisation and work hard to ensure acceptance of the vision. Investment in the development of staff is key. This includes staff appraisals and personal development plans, and ensures alignment of staff's inputs and outputs with the corporate objectives of the organisation.

Features of poor leadership include disengagement of the frontline staff from the board members, conflicting objectives and priorities, and high staff turnover, particularly those in leadership positions. Examples of this include Mid Staffordshire Trust, but also other trusts where there is evidence of poor communication, lack of transparency in decision making and focus on finance at the expense of quality. Trish feels in these cases there has not been enough emphasis at board level of assessing the skills and leadership of the team, nor evidence of meaningful board assurance.

Trish believes the ideal characteristics of a top leadership team include visibility, consistency, stability, flexibility and a good balance between business growth, improving quality and efficiency.

Trish estimates around 40% of health organisations have highly effective top team leadership. She feels the reason that some leaders fail to impact on making improvements relates to self-motivation, poor infrastructure, conflicting and competing priorities and poor development of leaders, both at personal and board level.

Trish believes improvements could be made if there was more investment in clarifying the organisation's purpose and vision, and staff were given greater freedom to progress the agenda. She feels there needs to be clearer accountability of all board members but particularly of chairs and chief executives for ensuring quality and safety of patients.

In terms of what needs to be done to improve quality in the front line Trish feels strongly that the implementation of statutory minimum nursing staffing levels is key. There is compelling evidence both internationally and in the UK that by increasing the numbers of registered nurses to patients safety and quality outcomes improve. This has been demonstrated in California, Australia and in some speciality areas such as critical care, paediatrics and midwifery in the UK. The recent success in reducing mortality and morbidity in stroke patients in London includes a mandatory ratio of one registered nurse to two patients.

Trish cites the example of UK midwives to birth ratios in some trusts falling well below the minimum standards as described in staffing tools, such as 'Birth rate plus'. Poor quality of care inevitably follows. The Care Quality Commission uses evidence from these types of tools/models to assess midwifery staffing levels, but similar standards in areas such as elderly care are not so easily accessed. Trish has been working with others on a project called 'Safe Staffing Alliance' where they are pushing for accessing the evidence that safe staffing levels matters and doing more work in areas where the evidence is less, such as community and mental health, to help introduce standards for all aspects of healthcare.

In Trish's experience some trusts have made significant progress in increasing nursing and midwifery staffing levels over the last few years, while others still need to make considerable investment and protect the continual identifying of nursing posts from cost improvement savings programmes.

Trish reflects on the current reasons for the resistance from government and also the recent Francis report (2013) in not taking the opportunity to compel organisations to implement minimum staffing levels. She believes this to be mainly about cost, which she thinks is a moot point, as the evidence shows clearly that increasing staffing levels has the effect of improving safety and quality and in doing so reduces patient harm, length of stay and costs. Trish's view is that if the citing of costs continues to be the main issue preventing the implementation of minimum nursing staffing levels more radical solutions may need to be considered, such as wide-ranging reconfiguration of hospitals to use staff more productively and effectively.

In addition to this Trish reflects on many of the initiatives that have been introduced, such as Leading Empowered Organisations (LEO) training and productive ward, aimed at supporting nursing leadership at ward management level and increasing the amount of direct nursing care given to patients. Trish feels strongly these programmes need to be accelerated, and increasing support given to ward staff such as enhanced administrative support would free up staff to spend more time with patients.

Trish talks about a number of research programmes she commissioned as Chief Nurse for London between service providers and higher education, which looked at a number of projects on how to attract and retain the best student nurses with a particular focus on the right emotional resilience, attitudes and values. These programmes are very significant pieces of work and show the importance of partnership between higher education and service providers. They are critically important to helping the new Local Education Training Boards develop and design future nursing programmes.

In terms of improving clinical engagement for medical leaders Trish believes that we need to take a fresh approach and avoid burdening them with perceived layers of bureaucracy, 'management speak' and endless meetings which can deter doctors seeking leadership positions in a trust. Instead Trish believes the key is to engage them in clinical leadership innovations such as reconfiguring stroke and vascular services as seen recently in London. Her belief is that engaging this leadership within trusts to lead and drive improvements in how clinical service are configured within their trust would be far more effective.

When selecting staff for key leadership positions Trish would look for evidence that the individuals' values mirror those of the NHS constitution. She would test for the individuals' understanding of personal accountability for quality and safety, and clarity of the purpose of the role for which they are applying. In addition to traditional selection processes Trish favours including patients and carers in the interview process, and also obtaining 360 degree feedback from the candidate's previous role. Trish is also very supportive of the executive leadership development programme, of which she has seen the results in a number of high-calibre candidates for director of nursing posts. Along with the LEO programme (which supports leadership of ward sisters/charge nurses) Trish believes strongly that funding needs to be secured and continued to ensure we are developing leaders for the future. Her views on the role of the NHS Leadership Academy is that it is early days, and there is potential to include more work on organisational culture, and also the types of evidence emerging from the research she has commissioned. She also believes it to be important that ward sisters/charge nurses are included in the programmes and that where possible these should be multidisciplinary.

In terms of ongoing monitoring of a leadership team's effectiveness, Trish advocates greater monitoring of a number of metrics by a range of stakeholders, including the trust board, the CCG and others. Examples of this include staff turnover, evidence of staff development, and patient feedback. Trish believes the work she previously led at the London Strategic Health Authority with the medical director, included some very effective models for monitoring safety and quality in trusts applying for foundation trust status. This included on-site peer review visits in addition to a table top review of key documents, providing comprehensive reports relating to each trust. The trusts visited received a clinical team who spoke to patients and staff and generated a detailed report of their findings. Trish's view is there is a need to further develop this type of clinical peer review as a means of sharing best practice and driving improvements.

Trish suggests that tests on healthy organisational culture could include asking frontline staff how often board directors engage with them, and then giving feedback regularly about what they believe to be good about the trust and what needs to be improved. Trish believes a framework for both selection and monitoring of leadership teams to be key, and feels that a tool to support this would be very useful.

Tom Sandford
Director, Royal College of Nursing, England

Tom joined the RCN in 1992 as a Policy Adviser. He then became a Regional Officer and London Regional Director before becoming Director of the RCN in England in 2004. Tom was previously general manager of mental health services in the London boroughs of Camden and Islington.

Tom trained as a general and mental health nurse and held a variety of posts in the fields of family therapy and acute and liaison psychiatry. He was Head of Professional Development in Bloomsbury Health Authority and was a member of the ministerial task force coordinating the development of the mental health national service framework. He has served on several public untoward incident inquiries and has taught mental health programmes at universities in Germany and case management programmes at the University of Barcelona.

Tom believes his success in his leadership positions has been facilitated through his interpersonal skills and emotional intelligence. He feels he is good at listening and fully analysing a situation before adopting a position or making a decision.

Tom believes that key features in leaders of successful organisations are integrity and courage; that is, courage to do the right thing which includes 'doing the difficult stuff'. He believes these leaders have high levels of energy and determination to drive through changes. These type of leaders don't get discouraged, or seek to blame when they encounter difficulties, instead they pick themselves up and continue to pursue the aims of the organisation. Tom feels this kind of energy is infectious to staff, who want to be a part of this drive, in particular middle managers in organisations who will feel motivated to energise frontline staff.

While this style of leadership sounds similar to that of the 'pacesetter', Tom believes the key difference is the presence of humility and being prepared to change their position if needed and when others advise.

Tom gives two examples of this, one is his previous chief executive Peter Carter (CEO/General Secretary RCN) whose energy and tenacity he admires. 'He gets up every day and gives 100% to the organisation no matter what obstacles he encounters.' Tom also cites his experience with those directors of nursing who demonstrate high levels of commitment to drive quality throughout the nursing service across their trust. He observes the way some nurse directors interact with and know their nursing staff, and who are totally committed to delivering the highest level of care and reducing harm. Tom visits many hospitals and can cite those that stand out; he says, 'You can feel the difference when you walk around the wards.' There is visible communication of the values of doing the best for patients each and every day and evidence of staff going the extra mile to maximise patient safety and design services to prevent falls and pressure ulcers and improve hydration and nutrition. The other significant thing he observes in these organisations is staff visibly enjoying their work. He states that there are many good trusts that he visits, but also some that don't demonstrate this same type of energy and commitment to want to be the best and to provide the safest care for patients.

Conversely the features of poorly performing organisations often demonstrate a lack of momentum, 'nobody leading' and a lack of integrity. Tom describes some leaders driving organisations in a dishonest way; what he means by this is they may articulate their commitment to improving quality and patient care, but they act in a way which results in the opposite. For example, they may achieve targets at the expense of the care of the patient. He also cites examples of where considerable investments have been made over the last few years into posts such as emergency physicians at considerable cost (around £100 000), but despite this investment these post-holders are rarely plugged into the day to day bed management teams nor actively working with the nurses managing the patient flow through the hospital. Poorly performing trusts rarely have every member of staff behind the leadership team to do their absolute best every single day for patients.

Tom estimates the number of health organisations with really highly effective leadership to be around 30%. Many more are good – but don't quite make the highly effective category. However, he believes that the NHS is fortunate in that it has a lot of value-based, committed managers.

The reason he thinks that many fail to make the necessary impact on driving quality is in part lack of experience, but it is also due to a lack of courage to highlight issues and problems. He feels that some directors of nursing don't have the courage to stand up to other executive colleagues, and sometimes there is a culture of not wanting to hear bad news. For some directors of nursing the consequences of speaking up may impact on them personally, and Tom doesn't underestimate how difficult this is. Tom reflects on his own role as a senior RCN director and says that he, too, can still find it difficult (even with his experience) to speak up in some organisations due to the reluctance to hear anything but good news, and that if this is his experience as an external visitor to a trust, he can fully understand the situation that some directors of nursing find themselves in.

Tom describes a number of situations he has encountered where nurses as a group either fail to deliver basic standards of care or work outside acceptable practice (e.g. groups of staff simply don't follow a medicine policy, or they cut corners). Tom feels there is something in the group behaviour that starts to normalise poor care. He finds it difficult to understand why nurses when they see poor care don't go to the director of nursing, or the RCN, but instead collude in continuing poor practice rather than challenging it. He doesn't just restrict this point to the nursing staff – there are also medical staff and others involved in these poor practices, either directly or indirectly, and they have responsibility for the patients under their care but in several high-profile examples, in the main they haven't put their head above the parapet.

Dr Andy Mitchell
Medical Director, NHS England (London Region)

Dr Mitchell joined NHS London in 2009. His has worked in the armed services and remains a civilian adviser to the Defence Medical Services. As Joint Service Clinical Director he was responsible for worldwide intensive care retrieval of sick children.

In 1997 he established the Central South Coast Paediatric Intensive Care network and chaired it through 7 years of development. In 2006 he began working as Associate Medical Director at Great Ormond Street, where he facilitated the London children's pathway group as part of the NHS Next Steps review.

He was a member of the London Clinical Advisory Group, and co-directs the Healthcare for London Children's project. He continues in part-time general paediatric practice. Dr Mitchell was appointed Medical Director for NHS London in April 2009, and was appointed to the Medical Director role in the London Regional Office, NHS England in 2014.

Andy attributes his success to his deeply held personal values which include a clear sense of purpose, integrity and honesty. He has a real passion for and commitment to ensuring the delivery of high-quality patient care and patient experience. His feels he has an intrinsic understanding of his own strengths and weaknesses and in being confident to appoint people around him with a range of skills that complement his weaknesses. He believes self-awareness and humility to be crucial features in successful leadership.

Andy likens successful leadership of organisations to that of 'good parenting' skills. He believes that partnerships and key relationships are essential within every team. He says there will always need to be a 'figurehead', but the team needs to exhibit features similar to those of a 'functional family' where there are intertwined relationships and the 'parents' need to exhibit behaviours and values that have the support of the whole organisation.

He believes the previous NHS London executive team to have shown many of these features, and there has been a strong feeling of mutual respect and a good balance of relationships between the team members, and as a result of this the team has delivered a huge amount for London. Looking across the trusts in London, some of them stand out as very successful, in particular some of the bigger teaching hospitals that are foundation trusts, but he observes 'that it is easier to be a good parent when there is money in the bank'. He adds there are also a number of smaller district general hospitals that he feels are quietly getting on demonstrating very good outcomes for patients.

Andy previously led work across London on developing the Organisational Health Intelligence Tool (OHI) which pulled together a number of measures such as mortality/morbidity, infection rates, patient experience and the like which were published quarterly. He also led the information revolution or 'transparency' project, putting more health information into the public domain. Alongside Trish Morris-Thompson, he led the safety and quality analysis of trusts applying for foundation trust status, which included commissioning clinical review teams to undertake site visits. Reflecting on these projects Andy feels that he has a good oversight of the trusts across London and that these measures, together with his meeting with the trust boards, give him a good 'feel' about where leadership is working well and delivering safer quality care, although 'safety' is a difficult concept to define with accuracy as it can be variable within any one organisation.

Where he sees poorly performing organisations he says there is usually evidence of fractured and dysfunctional relationships between board and executive members. This leads to the organisation becoming inward looking with a loss of focus on effective leadership. There is a lack of integrity and loss of focus on what matters in terms of safety and quality and a loss of 'caring' as a core value.

Reflecting on the Francis report (2013) he believes that some trusts lose their sense of purpose in terms of providing a quality service and get diverted by the delivery of financial balance and performance targets. He is concerned that performance targets are seen as an end in themselves, rather than a process to achieve quality. He supports the need for performance targets but feels strongly they need to be reframed in terms of driving quality improvement rather than ticking boxes.

The qualities Andy would look for in a medical director are authenticity, good communication skills, the ability to achieve wide engagement, and a deep understanding of the organisation. Ideally the medical leadership should be nurtured from within the trust as part of a succession planning programme, although there are occasions, particularly in large organisations, where external appointments are necessary. He finds the current pool of those putting themselves forward for the role is still relatively small in numbers. To become established as a medical director, credibility as a sound clinician is important. Clinicians are often reluctant to give up clinical practice, and feel that maintaining a clinical commitment is important. However, in most organisations the executive role with its increasing demands regarding quality requires at least 4 days a week, preferably with the support of a team of clinical leaders and administrative support constituting the 'Office of the Medical Director', with a clear remit, in conjunction with nursing colleagues, for quality improvement, quality assurance and dealing with failure in quality. Clinical time should be ring-fenced. The importance of the role of medical director in organisations needs more recognition, and training for the role is essential, as currently it is rather ad hoc, and in the past was virtually non-existent. He reflects on there being no curriculum for preparation for medical directors and thinks there will be a growing role for the Faculty in Medical Leadership and Management. He also sees a role for the NHS Leadership Academy, which he anticipates will be focusing more on wider corporate leadership. It will be important for these organisations to work together to ensure there is no duplication of effort.

The selection process for medical directors varies hugely; Andy is often invited to sit on interview panels and says they vary from a small panel to a 2-day full assessment centre approach, but he believes there needs to be a more consistent approach for these very important roles. He says that when there is a poor field borderline appointments are made and support is then offered via mentorship with another more experienced medical director. At times these have turned out to be successful appointments, but it is very dependent on how receptive the candidate is to reflection and accepting support. Andy would like to see this support more formalised for all medical directors and plans to set up a regular learning set to facilitate reflection and supervision.

Reflecting on the role that medicine has post Francis, Andy feels that while revalidation of doctors may have a lot to offer, a wider culture change is needed in medicine, starting with transparency, which includes clinical outcomes being in the public domain. He fully supports a duty of candour, and the need for a more honest dialogue with patients when things go wrong. He believes strongly that medical staff should be fully involved where investigations of serious incidents occur and reports should be shared with them.

There is currently wide variability of clinical practice across the UK, seen in terms of clinical outcomes, use of diagnostics, and thresholds for intervention. Andy believes the solution to this is absolute transparency and getting this information into the public domain. This will require courage from the medical profession, and while some will welcome this challenge others may find it difficult. He fully acknowledges that doctors are generally very good at navigating the system to access the best clinicians when it comes to their own families and he believes this should be a choice available to all of the patients accessing a service. Commenting on the concept of whistle blowing and raising concerns particularly about their own colleagues, Andy believes the solution lies in transparent data at trust board level which demonstrates variations in performance. He also feels that all consultants should be given very clear ground rules by the trust board about what is and isn't acceptable to the organisation, and direct them to the expected processes to raise concerns and report any incidents of poor quality care they observe.

The percentage of health organisations that Andy believes have highly effective leadership is below 50%, which even then may be optimistic, and he thinks there is much needed to improve the situation. Andy believes effective leaders need to be authentic, having a clear sense of purpose and demonstrating values and behaviour that motivate the staff to provide a more caring environment for patients. He believes investment is needed in quality improvement approaches, and this would engage staff in improving quality. There are many tools around, and he doesn't think it matters which methodology is used, but he believes there needs to be a huge shift in emphasis from that of performance management. Andy reflects on the work of IHI, and where some trusts have really embraced similar concepts of aiming for 'zero harm', 'no avoidable waits' and positive patient experience. His concern post Francis is there may be an increase in regulation and inspection, when what is really needed is a commitment to drive quality improvement as the top priority.

Reflecting on the decision the government took to commission Don Berwick from the United States to advise the British Government following the Francis report (2013), he very much welcomed this. He is a huge supporter of Don and the work he has led for the IHI and their commitment to health improvement, but he feels there are also many leaders in the UK who already have the skills to lead this. His concern is the 'bring in a saviour' mentality to help us save the NHS, a concept that continues to promote the charismatic leader as the answer, whereas the real answer lies in a leadership pioneering a culture change for the NHS, moving it from one of ticking boxes to one of commitment from the top to promote a service that puts caring at the centre of the health service.

Andy has mixed views about whether a framework would be helpful for selection and monitoring of leadership teams but acknowledges that there is a lack of consistency currently and wide variations in practice. He is not a great supporter of psychometric testing, but feels generally assessment centres add the degree of scrutiny to recruitment processes that are needed. He believes that panel members need far greater training and more time and resource needs to be directed to senior leadership appointments.

Andy's view about monitoring of organisations is that there needs to be a switch of focus which raises the profile of service improvement. He feels that previously at NHS London the work with OHI and safety and quality reviews provided good methodology for monitoring, but he is concerned about the capacity and capability for doing this following the demise of the SHAs. He thinks the clinical commissioning groups will need significant training and development to be able to fully undertake this role and will need support from the National Commissioning Board. He predicts there may be relationship tensions that develop between CCGs and trusts which will not be helpful in terms of their responsibilities as providers and the need to grow a quality improvement culture of caring. A collaborative approach to considering the whole of the local health economy and deriving the best outcomes for patients will be essential; unfortunately a rigid commissioner–provider split will tend to militate against this.

Andy thinks the focus of the National Trust Development Agency will be mainly on the foundation trusts pipeline, which will leave a significant gap if we are to address the number of trusts that are currently in difficulty. Andy believes that the Francis report (2013) exposed the ambiguity around accountability, compounded by the many layers of the NHS and external stakeholders involved. He feels strongly that defining who is accountable for healthcare failings needs to be explicit in the new arrangements post April 2013 when the new Health and Social Care Act (2012) comes into force.

Andy thinks that a framework for monitoring may be helpful, which focuses particularly on the clinical outcomes of the organisations and relationships both in and outside the Trust. He believes it is important to identify expected behaviours and measure specifically against them. Returning to his 'good parenting' analogy Andy says we need to be able to detect and take action against 'abusive parenting'. Staff grow and respond to a nurturing and supportive environment and steps need to be taken to ensure an organisational culture that engages staff in a vision of wanting to be the best rather than being told to be.

Andy is optimistic for the future, seeing a real opportunity to reframe healthcare and drive quality which will help organisations move away from punitive 'tick box' regimes. This will need to be led from the very top, and he hopes that the influence that Berwick has on the government with this an overall aim will lead to this being seen as the top priority.

Professor Hilary Thomas
Partner and Chief Medical Adviser, Healthcare Advisory and Global Centre of Excellence KPMG

Professor Hilary Thomas, MB, BS, MA, is a Fellow of the Royal College of Radiologists and a Fellow of Royal College of Physicians. Her PhD involved the biology of breast cancer. Hilary is KPMG's Chief Medical Adviser in the UK and a member of the Global Centre of Excellence in Health and Life Sciences.

Hilary is a past First Woman in Business Services winner and is a 2015 luminary of the Healthcare Businesswomen's Award. She leads KPMG's global health proposition, Care System Redesign, working across regional health ecosystems to redesign inter-organisational patient pathways and shift the provision of care to more appropriate settings. She has also led clinical engagement and clinical service redesign across several health economies, including in Singapore and the Netherlands, to deliver reconfiguration to ensure sustainable aligned services. Her passion is working at the interface of health and life sciences to redefine approaches and business models in a world of greater patient empowerment when facing long-term conditions and life-threatening diseases such as cancer.

Hilary qualified in 1984 and pursued a career in oncology from Senior Lecturer at Imperial to Professor of Oncology at the University of Surrey. She was an elected member of the General Medical Council from 1994 to 2003, during which time she chaired the committee on standards and medical ethics. After 23 years in the NHS she left in 2007 to become Group Medical Director of Care UK PLC before joining KPMG in 2009.

Hilary attributes her success to three key features: tolerance, resilience and accessibility. She believes herself to have an open mind and that being tolerant is an important leadership quality which has enabled her teams to flourish. She adds that she also had to be tolerant as a female leader 'to cope with the vicissitudes of being in a minority (most marked in the private sector)'. She feels that resilience has been very important, most of all in her medical director role at the Royal Surrey, at Care UK and getting through the partner process at KPMG. Hilary feels strongly that accessibility is key, and states that from her own 360 degree feedback it was clear that being accessible (and approachable) to the team are important for teams to be effective and empowered.

Hilary believes key features in the leadership of top performing health organisations include accessibility, visible leadership and being a 'learning and listening organisation' – one which examines what it does, evaluates it and learns from mistakes. This is particularly important for frontline delivery. She also feels authenticity and consistency of messages very important to build trust in employees. For clinicians this means humility, having an open mind and the ability to work beyond hierarchies and silos. It will also benefit from charisma and people skills as others – clinicians, patients and managers – will be more effectively engaged in this way.

An example given is that when Hilary was at the Royal Surrey an organisational development initiative entitled the 'Patient Line of Sight' was introduced which looked at the way in which patients experience the silos of a hospital, rather than the way in which the hospital is organised. This involved ward staff and key clinical staff across the organisation and began to address the culture of the organisation. It won the patient-centred care award of *Health Service Journal* and she felt this was 'great for developing our clinical leaders – nurses in particular. Sadly the key sponsor (CEO) moved on and his successor could not see the value of continuing the investment and so it did not become embedded.'

Hilary comments on the lack of freedom from external interference that executives need to deal with, and gives examples of systems in the United States where organisations feel more able to lead and to drive service change and improvements.

Hilary cites the past 5 years at Salford Royal Hospital as another excellent example where there are some very exciting developments. The chief executive at this trust has been in post for a number of years and has been very successful in terms of engaging clinicians in leading change and achieving high levels of patient and staff satisfaction.

Hilary feels that there needs to be a reward system for successful organisations such as these, and also link this to providing mentorship to other organisations where the executive teams are struggling. Hilary believes the current system of monitoring of trusts by external bodies focuses more on blame and punitive measures, where some executives are removed subsequently when there are serious problems, only later to be reappointed in other struggling organisations where the cycle may be repeated.

Hilary has been involved in recruitment panels for senior executives and feels there is sometimes pressure to appoint even when a candidate may be borderline in terms of what is required. She feels strongly that panels should 'only appoint the best' and where there is any doubt about a candidate they should not make a 'default' appointment even where repeating a recruitment process is likely to be long and resource intensive.

Hilary goes on to reflect on a number of organisations she feels have effective clinical leaders able to take the organisation forward at a much faster pace than organisations without leadership. She feels that medical directors who sit in their office, are nervous about having open and honest conversations and can't 'do difficult' will be hampered. There is also a need for professionalism and leadership development to equip those emerging or new leaders to step up and be and become more successful. The converse is also true and sadly she has observed far more organisations where the medical leaders are found wanting than the other way round – 'perhaps it's easier to recall the weaker than the stronger ones but it is depressing'. Hilary supports the appointment of full-time medical directors, her rationale being that these are very senior important jobs and require a significant time commitment. She believes that there are some specialities which make being a medical director very difficult, particularly where the consultant is leading a team. Hilary gives her own example when as an oncology consultant she found reducing clinical commitments to undertake a medical director role very difficult. She doesn't support the view held by some medical colleagues that the medical director should be elected by the consultant body, although they will need to be credible with them. She feels strongly that the medical director needs to have high-level communications skills, be visible, engaging and prepared to listen and take action where this would improve services for patients and staff.

Hilary contends that some of the key leadership features of poorly performing organisations include lack of consistency in messaging, lack of authenticity in terms of words and actions not being coherent and a 'bullying style and reputation in spite of great words in the weekly or monthly CEO communication!' Hilary states this is most clearly illustrated where there are often frequent changes of leadership so that organisations feel as though they are the issue – and that feeling permeates through how the staff feel about themselves.

Other features of failures in leadership can be seen where an organisation does not monitor its performance metrics – positive and negative – and therefore does not learn from its mistakes. Where a board does not have effective visibility of clinical performance metrics in particular they cannot run an effective organisation.

Hilary feels in terms of medical/clinical leaders at an organisational level there needs to be a cadre who are engaged with the management agenda and appreciate the need to improve efficiency and quality within the same or a reduced financial envelope. This requires leadership from clinicians, a willingness to hold up the mirror to colleagues and to have open, honest conversations. It also requires the individual not to default to 'being one of the pack'. Hilary says that sadly there are numerous examples in the NHS today – with about 20 trusts currently having interim CEOs, several having new CEOs every 1–2 years and others with difficulty appointing effective executive team members. However, the hallmark of a weak organisation seems to be the extent to which their clinicians (especially the consultants) are engaged in the day to day business of the organisation and feel it is their responsibility to deliver improvements, ensure that resources are well used and that the organisation continues to progress and innovate.

Hilary observes there to be many trusts across the country where there have been frequent changes of leadership – many of them are those with interim CEOs where there has been limited competition for the CEO post.

Hilary believes the ideal characteristics for a top leadership team include being open and honest in internal and external communications, the ability to have honest conversations with one another, and accessibility (e.g. an open door policy and being responsive to emails, phone calls etc.). She also feels that there must be challenge within the top team – in terms of its own development and also to continue to improve. She believes that 'good relationships between CEOs and medical directors can be game changers'.

Hilary estimates the percentage of health organisations that have highly effective top team leadership to be around 20%. She believes the reason why some leaders fail to impact on making improvements to direct care delivery is they 'stay in their office' and 'they don't connect with and consequently challenge clinicians'. These teams don't see the connectedness of money, efficiency and quality and so make short-term investment decisions which don't have an impact on the quality of care. They don't understand how to connect with the wider stakeholder group including patients and the public – to use this as a resource – and there is no consistency in their messages.

In terms of selection of top leaders Hilary would look for evidence of honesty, integrity, transparency, resilience, authenticity and communication skills, and application of these characteristics, similar to those criteria used within the CQC for assessment of a 'well led' organisation.

Hilary suggests considering role playing a difficult situation would be appropriate, and based on her own experience she reflects that 'having been put through my paces in this way at one NHS interview selection process and two within the private sector I found it very instructive! And I believe the panel did as well!'

Hilary feels that the NHS Leadership Academy will add value in terms of developing future service leaders. She feels this needs to include chairs and non-executives particularly as they are critical to the executive appointment process. Hilary would like to see greater attention in board appointments to a range of skills and style, and reflects that too often the same type of leaders are appointed who tend to favour more of a pace setter/autocratic style – 'get the job done' – than leaders who have a range of leadership styles and who appoint teams with a range of skills rather than characteristics similar to themselves.

Hilary is not confident that there is currently a pool of future leaders with the right skill set to take on the leadership of complex health organisations, and she believes the solution lies with more consolidation of hospitals and sharing proven successful leadership teams across a number of areas to drive improvements. She also feels mentorship of struggling chief executives needs to be developed and formalised to provide greater support where organisations are in difficulties.

In terms of ongoing 'monitoring' she would want to see the principles enshrined in the framework being adopted by the board and also evidenced through how performance is monitored and measured in the organisation and how this information flows up to the board and back down again – and how this is iterated by the board. In terms of clinicians in leadership positions the same characteristics should be sought. She says that 'sadly this does not appear to be the case very often'. However, there are promising signs that at least one country may have got it right with clinically qualified CEOs from Australia leading three of our top hospitals!

Dr Gordon Caldwell
Consultant Physician, Worthing Hospital, Western Sussex Hospitals NHS Trust

Dr Gordon Caldwell studied Physiological Sciences at Worcester College, Oxford, gaining a First Class Honours degree in 1974. He qualified as a doctor from King's College Hospital Medical School, London University in 1980, again with Honours. He obtained an MD from Oxford University in 1991.

Gordon worked at King's College Hospital, Brighton Hospitals, Edinburgh Royal Infirmary, The Hammersmith Hospital and Newcastle upon Tyne Hospitals, before becoming a Consultant in General Medicine with an interest in Diabetes and Endocrinology at Worthing Hospital in 1993. He is a Fellow of the Royal College of Physicians. He has been Clinical Tutor since 2000. Gordon has a particular interest in Quality and Safety at the Point of Care and in Leadership since attending the International Forum on Quality and Safety in Healthcare in Berlin in 2009. He has produced several publications focusing on the value of checklists in trying to control the complex, risky, error-prone processes of acute medical care.

He is married with two children and a granddaughter and lives in Worthing. He enjoys reading and travel, particularly skiing trips.

Gordon attributes his own success to his being 'full of ideas', perseverance, enthusiasm and a 'refusal to give up when faced with opposition'.

He believes key features of leaders of health organisations include having a belief in their staff, and spending a high proportion of time with the front line engaging with staff and patients. He feels strongly that leaders need to focus on action and processes, rather than papers and policies.

He cites a number of trusts he believes to be examples of good top team leadership, including Wigan Hospitals NHS Trust; Ashford St Peters and Gateshead NHS Trust. These examples are drawn from his experience over the last few years of having met some of their top teams and heard some of their presentation at a number of events, such as the BMJ and IHI International Forum for Quality and Safety in Healthcare.

He was particularly impressed with the work Gary Kaplan led at Virginia Mason Medical Centre in Seattle. He attributes their good reputations as being based upon his view that their chief executives really believe in empowering the frontline staff; they trust them and both encourage and give permission for them to innovate. They continually promote an improvement culture, and rather than being obsessed with cost cutting they recognise that if we focus on the core business, delivering the best high-quality care, within a lean structure and reducing duplication, the cost savings will follow.

He feels that some of the key leadership features of poorly performing organisations include finance ruling over quality, 'policies by the score with no change in processes' and a distant autocratic management team. Examples of these include 'nearly every NHS organisation he has dealt with over the last few years'. One example he gives of where doctors are continually instructed to focus solely on discharging patients to release beds, rather than the philosophy of ensuring right diagnosis, right treatment, right time, right place, right pace, right to no avoidable harm and Better Next Time (training and development). He says the importance of timely high-quality diagnosis and treatment and getting patients out of A&E in 4 hours has turned caring nurses into hard-hearted 'get the patient out of my department!' people.

He believes the ideal characteristics for a top leadership team include a clear, convincing commitment to high-quality, safe patient care, real openness – often seen on the shop floor – and a willingness to take risks. He feels that being respected by frontline staff is very important because of their clear personal involvement in the business of caring for sick patients.

Gordon feels the percentage of health organisations that have highly effective top team leadership is only 1%, and believes this is because so many leaders do not inspire, encourage, value or engage with the frontline workers, and they are risk averse and autocratic.

His view is that the majority of hospitals in the UK are 'medieval institutions with nice toys'. What he means by this is that these hospitals can do very advanced cardiac interventional procedures, or complex surgery, but they function in an out of date basic infrastructure which at times can't even tell you which consultant is responsible for a given patient's care. He compares it to a developing country where all the people seem to own a mobile phone but have no food, running water or infrastructures. He feels that if the health service were in charge of an airline they would never get the plane off the ground as it would be too weighed down with the number of staff collecting information on pieces of paper and trying to update each other.

He feels that many hospitals have hundreds of policies but spend little time on changing the processes to benefit patients. His fear is that the Mid Staffordshire public inquiry has simply added a burden of further regulation and paperwork without addressing the root cause of freeing up nurses and doctors to care for patients.

He believes that the junior doctors are the real hope for the future, and expresses disappointment in how the current consultant body has not been able to effect the changes needed. He feels the current hierarchy in medicine does not effectively use the juniors to their strengths, and in particular cites some of the graduate entry doctor trainees as having a wealth of experience, some having come from the business community and expressing frustration at how difficult it is to work in the hospital environment. They are surprised by how the structures and processes prevent change and opportunity to improve things for patients. His views about the lost opportunity to utilise the juniors more productively is illustrated by an example he heard at a leadership conference, where new business graduates in Singapore were given million pound budgets to manage when they qualified, 'and what do we trust our new graduate doctors? The job of handwriting hundreds of discharge summaries. We don't provide them with any kind of infrastructure or IT solutions to enable them to spend time with patients. Instead they end up spending hours on paper work when they should be treating patients.'

Gordon fully supported the former NHS Institutes' work on the productive nursing series Releasing Time to Care programme by freeing up nurses to nurse and spend more time with their patients, and believes the same could be done in medicine. He thinks that one reason there has not been a productive doctor series is probably down to the perception by the medical profession themselves that they don't need it, when in fact the opportunity to release doctors from administrative tasks is huge. He feels strongly that an awareness of the costs of medical time would be really beneficial. He has calculated that as a consultant he costs around £3–4 per minute, so 'when you calculate the cost of a group of doctors under-taking a ward round and spending up to 50 minutes to locate test results, missing notes etc., you can begin to see the real benefits in addressing some of the infrastructure issues'. He believes that if all doctors were pro-vided with a iPad-type tablet, where they can access all the information they need to care for the patients, it could save hours of time. Gordon feels this should go further and that patients could hold this information on their mobile phones. This works in other countries where the patient owns their own information, and it would also be safer, as one single record of the patient's medicines and recent tests (to avoid unnecessary repetition) would free up a considerable amount of doctors' and others' time. He also believes this could include the general practitioner's records of the patient, thereby reducing the need for such significant investment in hospital IT systems. His view is that outpatient clinics are running out of control and that freeing doctors from paperwork would reap many benefits.

Gordon also feels that patients should be aware of how much their care costs. For example, if they have had cardiac bypass surgery, he feels the patient's own discharge letter should include a breakdown of the costs, and if it has cost over £10 000, the patient should be able to judge whether that has represented good value for money. Gordon feels that operating in a free healthcare system should not prevent both patient and staff knowing the true costs. These systems are normal practice in other countries where patients are routinely billed for their care.

He believes that the health service should release leaders for a while into successful businesses, charities and the like to show them that com-plex processes need imaginative and inspiring leadership.

Gordon recognises that the management of doctors is not easy, and the job of the medical director is fraught with difficulties. He feels that the role is not an attractive one, and that not enough time is given for this role on top of clinical commitments. He is also not necessarily a supporter of full-time medical director posts either, but feels this can work if the post-holder possesses the credibility and the values to lead the medical workforce. The medical director has to be visible, approachable, understand the realities of frontline care and show real commitment to the delivery of high-quality care, and not be seen as pursuing targets above safe quality care. He feels it to be essential 'that medical directors can really relate to the front line and spend 70 to 80% of their time interacting with the front line rather than 70 to 80% in meetings and turning up only when things have gone wrong.'

The qualities he would look for when appointing to top leadership positions include evidence of being hard working, innovative, being keen to know everyone and to be seen as a listener, trusting people and specifically disliking lengthy paper work, policies and long-winded forms and slow processes. He particularly would value someone who is prepared to get 'their hands dirty on the job on a regular basis'.

Gordon believes the best predictor of future performance is past performance, so he would want to see evidence of actual achievements and the provision of reliable references. He adds that based on his reading of *Thinking, Fast and Slow* (Kahneman, 2011) that 'luck is a major factor in successful leadership'.

Gordon has worked for many years as a clinical tutor and has developed a framework for observation of effective leadership on ward rounds which has been seen as very innovative and valued by junior doctors (Caldwell, 2006). He believes the most important role in assessing doctors is to ask the simple question of 'whether they can do the job'. The way to answer this question is to observe them actually doing the job, and then feeding back to them to gain improvements. His concern about medical revalidation is that this does not include the observation of doctors doing the job. He believes it would be very simple to include real-time video of a short consultation with patients, but the constant concerns around the bureaucracy of gaining consent from patients (whom he feels would mostly be willing) gets in the way of a very simple innovative concept. He feels the same could be done with executive teams, who could be assessed on a number of measures, which may be linked to demonstration of values, culture, productivity, even down to the manner in which they chair a meeting.

CHAPTER 6

Confirming the diagnosis: what problems need to be addressed?

The views from the group of leaders presented in the previous chapter show considerable consistency with the management theories reviewed in Chapter 1. The majority of this group estimates the percentage of health organisations with effective leadership to be no greater than 50%, leaving around half requiring considerable support to make the improvements needed. The Francis report (2013) has led to speculation about how widespread problems may be. Evidence from a number of similar types of inquiries and reports suggest that despite a number of wide-ranging recommendations and action plans, these scandals have a tendency to be repeated.

To begin to address this, it is important to return to the question of the root cause, understanding why these failings continue to occur, before moving to answer what needs to be done. Simply generating a number of action plans based on such failings will not effectively address the issues, and risk continuing to repeat mistakes unless a more radical approach is taken.

Bringing together both the learning from the literature and the sounding from a sample of key leaders such as found here offers a more integrated approach in trying to address the issues.

TRUST BOARDS

The findings from both the sample interviewed and the literature are consistent in the view that failing organisations share a number of common features. In relation to failings of 'top teams' these include command and control leadership style, leaders 'who talk the talk but don't walk the walk', failure to address the key elements of culture, leading by anecdote instead of using sound data, denying there are problems, and refusing to hear or acknowledge problems and instead blaming individuals where failings occur. These teams have a closed culture, a 'silo mentality', a lack of authenticity, a bullying leadership style, and most importantly are 'lacking in integrity'. Most also mentioned a lack of vision, no clarity of purpose, and failure to communicate with staff – leading to employees being unsure of what were the organisational priorities.

Lack of engagement and visibility was also a feature, examples being where 'leaders stay in their office, don't respond to emails or phone calls, and don't connect with or consequently challenge clinicians'. Placing the chasing of targets and balancing the books above quality was mentioned by nearly all the group, and is a key feature of the recent Francis report.

The effective use of data and quality reporting were mentioned by a number of the group, in particular ensuring the boards are fully aware of the issues in their organisations and have the information with which to make decisions. The analysis from the Francis report shows both the board and the external stakeholders at Mid Staffordshire Hospital were provided with data and reports which should have acted as a huge warning that there were significant problems in the organisation, in particular the patient mortality data. The group highlight the importance of knowing the difference between reassurance and assurance and the importance of boards making decisions and taking actions based upon meaningful data.

There appears to be the view of a widespread practice of appointing senior leaders who are inexperienced and out of their depth. Sometimes organisations 'invest in one person who mistakenly thinks that their appeal to the workforce using personality or charisma is enough to hold a system together'. At its worst some chief executives 'can't cope with challenge and often take steps to remove individuals in a not very subtle way'. Frequent turnover of chief executives and executive teams appears to be a key feature of poor performing hospitals. These leaders may subsequently fail and be removed if there are serious problems (usually related to finance and failure to meet targets) only to be appointed to other struggling organisations.

Not infrequently it appears that the most challenged trusts attract the least experienced directors. Often these types of trust offer a lower salary and tend to appoint executive candidates in their first post, the result being the most difficult organisations being led by the least experienced teams. In terms of non-executives there appears to be huge variations in the calibre of the post-holders, and the support they have from their chairs; these posts are key to these health organisations in terms of assurance and governance. Lord Hunt makes the point that we pay chairs and non-executives of non-foundation trusts less and '. . . it is not surprising that these types of organisations often fail to attract and recruit high calibre experienced staff'.

NURSING LEADERSHIP

The last few successive governments have failed to demonstrate their acknowledgment of the importance of senior nurse leadership being represented in both government and various layers of the health service. Examples of this include the campaigns the RCN has led around ensuring the position of the chief nurse at the Department of Health, strategic health authorities, foundation trust boards and more recently membership of the senior executives' roles of clinical commissioning groups. Baroness Emerton supports this, speaking of the importance of 'raising the profile of nursing at governmental level'.

It is clear from the previous Francis report (2010) that there is much confusion around the role of the director of nursing. Within trust boards they hold roles of accountability for professional nursing standards but at times with a perceived lack of direct authority over the line management of nurses, which is usually the role of the director of operations or the chief operating officer. This means the director of nursing needs to have very high level influencing and negotiating skills. Many of the group interviewed talked about the need for executives to have 'courage' and to be engaged in more than just nursing. A number of the group highlighted the lack of visibility of directors of nursing and other executives as an issue, with most believing that all members of the executive team should be very visible to frontline staff.

The nursing care described in Francis (2013) is distressing to read and it is difficult to comprehend the circumstances which would lead to staff acting in such a way. This is an area which needs far greater research, and some of the group talked about this in more detail. While it appears clear that there were some individuals involved in the 2013 Francis inquiry whose practice goes so far outside acceptable standards they should not be permitted to remain on the nursing register, there were many others (nurses and other staff) who were guilty by omission and failure to act and raise concern as bound by their professional codes of practice and their employment contracts.

The low levels of nursing staff and in particular the ratio of registered to non-registered nurses is a key issue within the Francis report. Liz Robb (2013) in an article published in *Nursing Times* further highlights the issues of nursing staff shortages and the associated low registered staffing level resulting in poorer quality care. She does not accept the view that nurses have lost compassion or their ability to care and makes the point that compassion costs, in terms of time, energy and emotional effort; being unable to meet the demands of their patients and leaving work undone carries an enormous burden for caring nurses. It is recognised that when nurses become overloaded this can result in burnout and at its worst a loss of humanity. This does not in any way seek to excuse the accounts of appalling care received by the patients at Mid Staffordshire, where there is no doubt that immediate action needs to be taken. Liz's point is about seeking to understand fully the circumstances and context which allows such poor care to occur and to target specific action at the root cause which includes ensuring minimum staffing levels, below which no ward would ever fall.

The need for nurses to be given more time to care was highlighted, and examples of many of the initiatives such as LEO courses, productive ward, and other programmes have a tendency to be discontinued without evaluation of impact. The need for ward sisters/charge nurses to have bespoke leadership training is also a very important point.

Francis (2013) recommended the need for ward managers to be freed up from other duties to supervise staff, and also to ensure that ward rounds by doctors all include a registered nurse. Gordon Caldwell's evidence to the Francis inquiry showed the results of an audit in his own trust where the percentage of nurses accompanying doctors on ward rounds needed significant improvement. Berwick (2012) at the IHI conference in Auckland highlighted the importance of nurses (and other members of the multidisciplinary team) being part of ward rounds.

MEDICAL LEADERSHIP

The limited time given to the important role of medical director on top of clinical commitments is mentioned by some of the group, with mixed views about whether this should be a full-time position. Similar issues are mentioned about the lack of visibility and poor engagement of the clinical workforce. It appears that while the government (and healthcare policy in general) continues to place medical staff into top leadership positions, there is both a lack of capability and capacity to fulfil such roles. Effective preparation for these roles is essential and some of the group mentioned the potential of leadership development and mentorship programmes.

Another important aspect for doctors is addressing the burden of paperwork, and lack of information technology infrastructure to reduce duplication and free up doctors to give more time to their patients. The value of initiatives such as the previous work on the productive series being relevant to doctors is raised by Gordon Caldwell as also a way to help manage the daily grind of endless emails and meetings, and excessive administration.

Tom Sandford makes an interesting point where he has observed the increased investments in emergency medicine consultants which bear no relationship to the day to day management of 'the beds', instead leaving such an important aspect of hospital flow to the nurse managers. Nurse managers are expected to manage the flow of patients with at times little support from doctors, and then be on the receiving end of criticism about caring more about targets than patients.

Examples given where leadership in medicine has been more successful are seen in larger scale strategic projects such as the stroke strategy for London, and leading hospital reconfigurations in pursuit of improved health outcomes. It appears that medical leaders are able to be more influential where they are leading from a clinical perspective, but currently this is not particularly visible within hospital settings. Addressing this must surely be the key to ensuring that doctors feel they have a strong voice and lead change, particularly where they have concerns about standards of care. Working in partnership with directors of nursing within top teams is essential, as responsibility for improving standards is a whole board accountability. Medical directors and clinical directors will need to demonstrate effective leadership across their organisations and fully embrace the need to drive clinical innovation and improvement.

The point made by Gordon Caldwell regarding awareness of costs is an important one, but it is not only the patients who need to be aware of health costs; doctors are heavy spenders of the budget, and as such have a huge responsibility to the public as taxpayers to use resources in the most effective way. Providing medical leaders with accurate information about expenditure is key, as it their responsibility in areas such as procurement of medical equipment, ensuring an evidence base for ordering tests and procedures and not overdiagnosing and overtreating patients. To be effective in this requires a far more engaged clinical leadership than is currently present in today's hospitals.

CHAPTER 7

What needs to be done about effective leadership to help cure the NHS?

In seeking evidence for the diagnosis of what may be going wrong in potentially up to 50% of UK health organisations, it becomes possible to begin to construct a framework based on the literature and the experience of the top healthcare leaders interviewed.

TRUST BOARDS

Baroness Emerton probably best sums up the views of the top leader group when she states that top teams 'should never lose sight of the family/patient needs' and know how to 'be a good team player ... use influence ... know how to balance education, experience of practice, be politically aware and have wide understanding of context'. Leadership needs to articulate a compelling vision, engaging all staff, have energy, commitment, clarity of objectives and priorities and the ability to translate and connect with frontline staff. Visibility and credibility were also mentioned by many of those interviewed; others mentioned courage and resilience as being important features of leaders. The evidence suggests that no leader can be expected to be expert in all areas and the importance of self-awareness of the individual and the team is key to recognising and actively managing the strengths and weaknesses of the team. The distributed leadership model of the Tricordant approach (as explained by Roger Greene) categorises the importance of undertaking a diagnosis of the balance of skills in the team and of identifying gaps and actively recruiting individuals with the right skill set to complete the leadership team.

The importance of values and culture is common to both the literature and the views of the leaders, many highlighting the importance of the behaviours and actions of the leadership teams and how these are perceived by the frontline staff.

It is important to be able to attract high-calibre candidates to chairs of trust board positions as these are very senior leadership roles which carry high-level accountability for patient safety and quality. The current remuneration system needs to be reviewed and a more consistent approach taken for both chairs and non-executive roles. The current pay system varies between trusts, with foundation trusts being free to pay non-executives more, and it is therefore difficult to attract experienced chairs to lead the more challenged non-foundation trusts. It is also necessary to better equip chairs of boards with the skills they need for their leadership and accountability roles. A review of the time required for the role of chairs and non-executives is also required, as most have limited time to undertake their role and focus their activity. A large percentage of their time is taken up with meetings and chairing committees. While this is important it is also vital they engage with leadership and frontline staff at all levels of the organisations outside of formal meetings. It is also important to create opportunities for them to meet with patients as individuals on the wards and also in various patient and carer user groups. Fully aligning the role of the non-executives with the organisation's clear objectives and priorities would then help in determining their role and purpose and the way in which their time is best allocated. A more consistent approach to defining the roles of board secretaries would also help. These roles can be highly supportive of chairs and non-executives, but at present they are not consistently in post throughout healthcare trusts. Where these posts do exist there is a variety of job descriptions, grades and training available for the roles. Current experience suggests huge variations across trusts even to whether they have these roles at all. Developing and standardising board secretary roles is key to supporting non-executives in delivering their role.

A bespoke development programme needs to be an integral part of the NHS Leadership Academy and include chairs, non-executives and board secretaries. There is also the potential to further develop and improve the current appraisal system for chairs and non-executives supported by the academy.

CHIEF EXECUTIVES AND EXECUTIVE TEAMS

The evidence from the literature, supported by the views of those interviewed, suggests that to select the best top team leadership far greater attention needs to be given to the selection and ongoing monitoring of these very senior posts. These are highly paid positions with high levels of accountability and responsibility for the lives of the patients and the working environment of staff, and yet the approach to these appointments can vary from full-blown recruitment centre assessment via a recruitment company to a single interview with a small panel where at times there may also be a low-calibre pool of candidates. Lord Hunt states: 'We pay execs huge amounts of money, but the length of time chief execs remain in post is often short and when they get into some kind of difficulty they are removed.' Hilary Thomas illustrates this point where she says that at times 'there is pressure to appoint even when a candidate may be borderline in terms of what is required'.

Many of those interviewed advocated the needed for multi-day assessment centres as an integral part of any selection process but none supported the use of psychometric testing in the way currently delivered.

The NHS Leadership Academy/Health Education England has great potential for supporting a more rigorous and standardised approach to leadership appointments based upon NHS leadership characteristics, but this will require significant investment in training those who sit on panels.

There may also be the need for a much tougher interviewing process such as seen in the BBC series *The Apprentice*. In one of the episodes the final candidates undergo a very complex gruelling process, being interviewed by four separate senior *executives* (selected by Sir Alan Sugar). They scrutinise the candidates' CVs and ask very probing questions; notes are compared at the end of the day. There are some similarities to this approach seen in some assessment centres, and some head-hunting companies offer a service of screening out applicants in similar ways, but it could be argued that few executives have been fully trained in these types of techniques. While many will be familiar with the NHS leadership framework, fewer will be effectively skilled to be able to probe and test for evidence of attributes during the selection process.

There is an urgent need for a consistent process and framework to guide selection of executives and to aim for consistency of approach across the NHS. Selecting the best and protecting organisations from selecting and promoting the wrong individuals for leadership positions are essential to avoid appointing individuals who may be incompetent, manipulators or bullies (Organ, 1994; Clarke, 2005). Protecting organisations from this includes looking for evidence of leadership attributes than include transparency and communication of strong ethical values. In combining the experience of the top healthcare leaders and the literature the following approach is proposed. (The tool kit/framework summarises the following points in Appendix B.)

SELECTION OF EXECUTIVES

When recruiting executives the chair of the team needs to undertake a detailed analysis of the current team (recognising theories on stages of decline, and incomplete leaders – Ancona *et al.*, 2007; Collins, 2001) and identify deficits. There needs to be clear agreement on the organisation's core purpose: safety, quality and values articulated which reflect the behaviours expected in the organisation. This needs to be followed by the development of detailed job descriptions, explicit in areas of leadership, values and engagement. The job advertisement needs to be very clear on expectations of the individual, and values and behaviour required.

Once applications are received, there needs to be detailed scrutiny of the CV, checking evidence of qualifications and track record, which includes verifying these with employers from the previous 5 years. The selection process should also seek evidence of 360 degree feedback which includes frontline staff from the applicant's current post (while recognising the limitations of this approach). Once short listing is completed and the candidate is invited for interview, the process needs to include objective independent testing of evidence for values, integrity, vision, self-awareness, learning, intellectual/political capacity, ability to cope with change, ability to make difficult decisions, courage, willingness to receive challenges, and evidence of personal exposure to challenges. There also needs to be testing of leadership levels, recognising the need to avoid appointing the level 1 or level 2 leaders described by Maxwell (2011). This process needs also to include observation/case studies of the applicant in their current work setting and scrutiny of evidence of organisational achievements.

The interview panel needs to be highly skilled and include members who have received training, have effective listening skills and the ability to critically evaluate responses, and be alert for charm/charisma (which can influence members of the panel). Part of the process should include asking the candidate on the day of the interview for a three or four-page statement about their achievements, the reasons they want the job and their work ethic. The interview questions need to focus on: ethical values (what does it mean to do the right thing for the right reason?); relational values (how would they build an environment of trust and respect for others?); and success values (what goals do they believe are worth spending their life on?) (Clarke, 2005).

Seeking references is an essential part of the process; it is important to seek views that gain evidence of positive values such as those determined in the person specification. However, Clarke (2005) recommends asking specific questions relating to the applicant's previous workplace which include any examples of manipulative behaviours, suggestions of unprofessional behaviour and any examples of intimidating behaviour which includes asking whether the candidate has 'ever lost their temper for short periods of time to make people afraid of him'. There is a real need to be this specific in questions to avoid appointing (and potentially reappointing) leaders with sociopathic characteristics.

This process can be adapted for all level of leadership positions. It is as important to select only the best ward sisters/charge nurses, consultants and other leaders as it is board members. While this process appears lengthy and possibly resource intensive, these are very senior roles and there is sufficient evidence both in the Francis report (2013) and from the views of those interviewed that significant improvements need to be made. It also is important to note the subsequent resources needed when poor appointments are made.

MONITORING THE EFFECTIVENESS OF LEADERSHIP TEAMS

There is a variety of external processes currently in place which aim to assess, measure and support board leadership. The regulator Monitor specifically requires this of trusts seeking foundation trust application; previously strategic health authorities undertook trust visits and where necessary full reviews. This is also part of the role of the CQC, commissioners of services, and a range of external stakeholders such as the royal colleges. Some trusts undertake their own board development sessions or commission experts in the field to support them. Despite this it is clear from both the recent findings of the Francis report and from those interviewed that there may be fewer than 50% of healthcare organisations in the UK with highly effective leadership, and some urgent action needs to be taken to address this.

There is a need for all senior leadership teams to undertake an honest appraisal of the strengths and weaknesses of their members. The team needs to be clear about their core purpose and structure their board portfolios to ensure they have the right balance of skills across the team. They need to recognise the theory of 'distributed leadership' and give themselves permission to acknowledge the concept of the 'incomplete leader'. As Roger Greene states, 'it is the norm for leaders to be incomplete and self-awareness of their weaknesses is essential for there to be a balance of skills in any leadership team to build on strengths and offset weaknesses'. The model proposed by Tricordant is specifically designed to build on this concept and remove 'reliance on the heroic and charismatic model of leadership'.

Undertaking this diagnostic process is critical for the team to undergo before they start to generate objectives and agree priorities. The key is to ensure that the structure of the team and the organisation supports the core purpose, which in healthcare should always be about the delivery of safe, quality care to patients. Roger Greene raises an important point regarding how trust boards are currently structured. Greater attention needs to be given to infrastructure, with a review of how boards could be better structured for more effective delivery.

It appears that many of the most successful NHS organisations share some common features, one of which is a stable top team, particularly with senior executives having been in post for some years. A number of the more challenged trusts appear to have a rapid turnover of executives, with often the most challenged failing to attract a good field of candidates, or making borderline appointments. The attrition rate of chief executives is very high, and there needs to be a formalised support system in place.

A formal mentoring programme needs to be set up for new chief executives (and teams), pairing them with the most successful and experienced and using examples such as those of head teachers being seconded to run failing schools. A similar approach of seconding a more experienced and effective chief executive into challenged trusts needs to be considered. Organisations with the most effective leadership will also have effective succession and deputising arrangements, which would enable the development of deputies to act in chief executive roles, releasing the chief executive to support a challenged organisation in making the improvements needed. Other benefits of this approach include the sharing of good practice and building confidence in troubled organisations. Other options include trust mergers and acquisitions, which may have the potential to raise the calibre of leadership teams, but also bring uncertainties and at times political and local opposition.

All of those interviewed supported the need for more effective monitoring of leadership teams, most supporting many of the methodologies used such as peer review processes currently in place. The challenge that Francis (2013) gives is how such failings as those seen at Mid Staffordshire Hospital could occur when all of the external stakeholders' peer review processes were already in place. There appears to be a distinct lack of coordination and bringing together data of what is known about organisations in a more meaningful way. Previous work undertaken by SHAs is now undertaken by the CCGs and NHS England. Peter Carter, in his interview, is concerned whether the CCGs have the experience to do this and believes the system to be confusing as to where this responsibility will sit, and, he says, 'with so many organisations in difficulty this is a huge worry'.

DATA AND PERFORMANCE

One solution needed is the development of a common set of data and quality indicators agreed nationally, with some room for local ownership with the CCGs, which includes reports from the wide range of external stakeholders. Currently there is wealth of data (both hard and soft) available to trusts and their stakeholders. Trusts generally spend a large amount of time collecting data on their organisation with the main purpose of providing this to external stakeholders, often termed as 'feeding the beast'. What is needed is far greater analysis and use by the trusts of their own data, interpreted for their own board assurance. There still tends to be a bias towards using red, amber, green (RAG) ratings for looking at performance, which carries the risk that board members focus their attention only on those in the red categories. It is far more useful to use run charts and track progress/deterioration of performance; these have been fully adopted by IHI (Berwick, 2012), who advocate using data to track variability and seek real causes for variability of quality over a period of time. The power of meaningful data supports effective decision making and is essential to trust boards. Some of the data that trusts can capture includes softer data, case study observation, feedback from patients in the form of narrative, and reports from royal colleges on specific services. Coordinating, analysing and interpreting this data and presenting it in a meaningful way is a complex task and will require allocation of resources in trust governance teams and board secretaries to ensure this is undertaken. Frontline staff need to be able to recognise and own their own data and be free to use it to drive frontline improvements to patients.

Benchmarking data can be very useful but is also fraught with areas of variability, particularly when comparing different types of hospitals. Ranking performance such as the national patient and staff surveys may also not be helpful. Ranking will always ensure there is a best and a worst on the bell curve distribution. What would be more useful is to agree a standard benchmark; for example, ensuring that over 85% of patients will be satisfied with their care, or that 85% of staff would recommend the trust as a place they would want their relative treated. The important point is for the organisations to believe this would be their absolute minimum standard, and the core objectives of the trust and therefore all staff would be for this to be achieved. This then becomes more meaningful than meeting a government target. A lot of criticism has been levelled at the government targets such as the 4-hour wait in A&E, in that it has in some way affected how staff behave and change their priorities, and it has unintended consequences. Translation of the performance target is a key role for the trust board.

ROLE OF THE LEADERSHIP TEAM

It is the leadership team's absolute responsibility to communicate the quality priorities to staff and ensure that all care is directed and supporting the aim of high quality, which in turn supports productivity and best use of resources. Their role is to determine the values of the organisation and define what is important to it. They need to be clear on what the organisation stands for and be explicit about what they believe 'is and is not acceptable' to the organisation. To achieve this they need to engage the whole organisation, which is about engaging the workforce, who will need to own and live the values at every level. This becomes an easier task if a highly effective leadership team is in place that demonstrates all of the principles of a learning organisation (Senge, 1990).

Some of the group interviewed spoke about work currently ongoing on the concept of a 'culture barometer'. This was mentioned by both Liz Robb and Baroness Emerton who have been working on piloting a tool with a small number of organisations. This work post Francis will inevitably grow, and will need significant funding to support its rollout; it is also an area that the NHS Leadership Academy could further support as part of its development. Any method of testing organisational culture needs to start with careful definition of the standard that will support successful auditing. There are also ways in which trusts can support this type of work; for example, they could speak directly to frontline staff and ask them some simple questions and give feedback regularly on what they believe to be good about the trust and what needs to be improved. They can regularly present stakeholder reports about the leadership; there are many undertaken by various medical colleges: student nurse evaluations about their placements, junior doctors' feedback to name but a few. Many of the group interviewed mentioned 360 degree feedback. While this is a useful tool, it can have limitations and be subject to bias. Bullying cultures in particular can be difficult to detect this way if staff feel concerned that they may be identified if they speak openly and honestly.

The future role of the Royal College of Nursing was raised in the Francis report (2013), drawing questions of the perceived conflict between the professional and trade union arms of the organisation. This will no doubt be the subject of future debate, but a number of the royal colleges including medical and midwifery hold a large amount of data about each organisation. The RCN regional offices support local RCN members in the various health organisations in their patch, which means they have a considerable amount of data that will relate to the organisation's behaviours. For example, some trusts have a lower threshold for disciplining staff (e.g. for a drug error) than others, some impose major service changes or staffing reductions without sufficient consultation, some hold data on grievances, and so on. Sharing this information in the form of an annual report to the trust could prove really useful to the board in terms of assessing organisational culture and in stimulating change.

Whistle blowing is another area that has been highlighted in the Francis report and is a feature of many previous healthcare reports of failings. Most if not all healthcare organisations have policies in place that support staff to speak out, but the actual experience of raising concerns via this route has been shown to be very difficult if not impossible for some. This situation is by no means unique to frontline nurses, as even the most senior nurses may have the same fear. Many of those interviewed spoke of the need for directors of nursing to have courage to raise these issues, but acknowledged that at times the DONs have been overruled or removed rather than the issue being addressed effectively.

The recent experiences of those that have 'whistle blown' in relation to Mid Staffordshire have been well documented in the press. Protection for staff will no doubt now be strengthened, but there is also a wider range of staff from all disciplines who need to take responsibility for speaking up when they witness poor care. For every case of neglect or harm to patients on the wards of Mid Staffordshire from nursing staff, there will have been a range of other health professionals present on those wards every day. These include the medical teams, therapy staff, pharmacists, chaplains, volunteers, and catering and cleaning staff, all of whom have a responsibility to raise concerns. Effective leadership teams need to ensure every member of staff has a mechanism for raising concerns, and that these concerns are acted upon. Too many staff across the NHS have returned staff surveys stating they would not wish their relative to be cared for in their hospital, but it is not clear what steps they have taken to address this. This should be an additional question in the survey.

NURSING

Without doubt the impact of the inquiry into Mid Staffordshire has seriously damaged the status of the nursing profession and there is a need to respond collectively to this challenge and address this issue. This will require the profession to fully acknowledge and understand what has gone wrong. The context in which nursing operates is important and there are a number of contributory factors which have led to this situation, including political, economic and social influences. That said, there is much that the nursing leadership needs to do for itself and this will require great courage and commitment as well as the support and engagement of the whole nursing profession.

There needs to be a recognition of the context in which nursing operates, both politically and culturally, and how this can be addressed. Francis (2013) has been clear about the need for greater representation of nursing at all levels and in particular at government level. The government needs to recognise and take action on the importance of ensuring senior nursing leadership and advice at policy level. The Francis report has the potential to be very empowering for nursing, and senior nurses in particular will need to step up and ensure their voice is heard and that patient safety is always seen as the top priority for all health organisations.

There needs to be a review of the international learning about nursing, as other countries, such as the United States and Australia, have addressed similar problems. There needs to be a movement to urgently progress legislation for minimum registered nursing staffing levels and protecting registered nursing and midwifery numbers. This would mandate providers, support health professionals in maintaining standards, inform tariff development, and more importantly protect the patients and keep them safe. There continues to be reluctance from governments (from all political parties) to accept the arguments for legislating for minimum staffing levels. The RCN has a significant role and huge opportunity to take centre stage in professional leadership for nursing and it should be leading the work on nursing staffing levels. However, when the National Institute for Health and Care Excellence was given the role of evaluating the research and publishing guidance there was huge optimism that this would help to increase staffing levels in hospitals, underpinned by robust evidence. Sadly it appears that the cost of implementing safe staffing levels hit significant political resistance at a time of economic pressure and it remains to be seen if the reality of agreeing minimum staffing levels despite international evidence will ever be realised for the NHS.

There needs to be further leadership development for nurse leaders at all levels and to ensure they are represented at all levels of healthcare. This does not necessarily need to be just in terms of programmed courses, but should include secondments and shadowing opportunities. There also needs to be an expansion of programmes such as offered with the Florence Nightingale scholarships which are self-directed but include support and wider opportunities to network and make connections outside of the nursing profession.

Leaders in nursing need to know how to effectively promote, deliver and evidence improvement, which allows good practice to be shared and spread where improvements for patients are achieved and tangibly demonstrated. There is also a need for nurses to develop skills in technology and the use of digital tools to support nurses and nursing care. There needs to be a comprehensive impact evaluation of the range of previous initiatives which have been implemented; examples include the Leading Empowered Organisations course, productive ward initiative, and point of care. Many of these were felt to be effective but required continued funding and commitment, yet too often instead they have been replaced with the 'next initiative'.

Visibility and ensuring that staff not only know their senior nurses but feel able to engage and raise concerns is essential. Some directors of nursing have very wide portfolios or cover a large number of sites which can often result in competing priorities, and so they need to find ways to increase their time engaging with the front line. One solution could be to introduce planned formal clinical sessions as part of the role in a similar way to that of the medical director. This should also include senior nurses in commissioning roles with responsibility for a number of organisations.

Geography and time can provide challenges, but allocating dedicated clinical time within these roles needs to be a priority.

There are many examples of where directors of nursing have introduced the concept of clinical days, and some have extended this to include senior nurses at all levels. However, this needs the support of the whole executive team and to be seen by the organisation as a priority. There also needs to be a careful balance between being visible in the clinical area and empowering ward managers, matrons and other senior nursing staff who have the day to day direct responsibility for their areas. As a minimum all of the directors (including the non-executives) of the board should commit to meeting with patients and carers on at least a weekly basis. Some methods include pairing of non-executives with directors and allocating a group of wards to them. This then gives opportunities for direct feedback to the board to improve ways of ensuring the patients' voices are heard.

Formal revalidation has been introduced for nursing but unfortunately not with anything approaching the level of funding per head as the medical profession has received, despite nursing having a far greater workforce in terms of numbers. Time will tell whether the so-called 'proportionate' approach by the NMC gets near to achieving what was envisaged when Francis recommended this in his report.

There also needs to be significant investment in post-registration/graduate education and alignment with funding of similar levels to that seen in medicine. To date there has been huge inequity in the allocation of funding; the established local education and training boards (LETBs) will need to address how funds can be more effectively distributed in the context of the current economic climate.

There needs to be a re-energising of nursing research to promote evidence-based practice both in clinical care, leadership and organisational learning. Some of the research projects commissioned by Trish Morris-Thompson are good examples of where research can contribute to addressing many of the issues raised within the Francis report. It is important to raise the profile of higher education, bring together the work of all the nursing faculties across the UK and recognise the huge contribution they can make towards addressing many of these issues.

MEDICINE

The role and time allocated for the medical director in trusts needs to be reviewed. There are mixed views about whether these should be full-time posts, with pros and cons expressed by some of those interviewed. To be effective, these roles need more time allocated and the role needs to be effectively aligned with the rest of the executive team and directed to ensuring the delivery of safe, quality care to patients. Similar attention needs to be given to the role of clinical director if the clinical leadership is to be improved. Both these roles are not currently seen as attractive by many and there is often a failure to attract highly skilled candidates to apply for the posts.

The role of the medical director will need to explicitly include accountability for mortality and morbidity of patients, and effective job planning. This includes ensuring that all consultants are supported in taking full accountability for the patients in their care, and that ward rounds are coordinated and supported by nurses and other members of the multi-disciplinary teams. They will also need to be leaders in terms of advising on future reconfigurations of services, and advising on contract negotiations when outsourcing services such as pathology, radiology and others.

The required characteristics of effective leaders apply equally to medical directors. They specifically require courage to do some of the more difficult things that may not have the support of their colleagues. Hilary Thomas states the 'need for professionalism and leadership development to equip those emerging or new leaders to step up and be and become more successful'. Much greater attention needs to be given to the development of consultants for these roles. While they are usually highly skilled, consultants may find that they are relatively inexperienced in the reality of working at executive level, and are overwhelmed by the layers of bureaucracy and numbers of meetings and emails. This point was supported by

Trish Morris-Thompson who 'believes that we need to avoid burdening them with perceived layers of bureaucracy, "management speak" and endless meetings which can deter doctors seeking leadership positions in trusts'.

Realising the benefits of revalidation is an enormous challenge which has the potential to overhaul the way in which medicine is currently practised. Feedback from patients and clinical outcomes as an integral part of appraisal will begin to help address some of the failings identified in the Francis report.

Doctors must speak up when they observe or suspect poor standards of care; this includes at times raising concerns about their colleagues, and spans both primary and secondary care. It also includes GPs, who have a responsibility to highlight concerns if their own colleagues' practice falls below acceptable standards. Systems need to be in place to formally evidence concerns (avoiding anecdote) and to be confident that such concerns will be acted upon.

In terms of engaging the clinical workforce this needs urgent attention and a fresh approach is needed. The key is to engage them in clinical leadership innovations such as reconfiguring stroke and vascular services as seen recently in London (and highlighted by Trish Morris-Thompson). Engaging this leadership within trusts to lead and drive improvements in how clinical services are configured within their trust would be far more effective. There is a need to develop a specific strategy to actively engage lead clinicians using the six-phase framework described by Reinertsen *et al.* (2007) which includes: discovering common purpose; reframing values and beliefs (e.g. patients being partners in their care); agreeing a plan; supporting the implementation of the plan; showing courage (up to the board level); and adopting a leadership style that supports engagement. The level of medical engagement can be measured by the board by assessing the number of doctors who will consistently say positive things about their organisation, intend to stay and practise in the organisation and strive to achieve above and beyond what is expected in their daily role (Bohmer, 2012).

Leadership development needs to be undertaken at all levels, and actively engaging junior doctors is very important. Often these doctors have the benefit of 'fresh eyes', and by working in a number of trusts they are able to very quickly assess where improvements can be made. As such they need a forum to be able to provide feedback on their observations, and also to ensure they understand their accountability in raising concerns where they feel care of patients is lacking.

A productive medicine module based on the nursing ones (designed by the NHS Institute) needs to be developed and introduced for hospital-based doctors. The aim is to free up doctors to allow them to spend more time with patients, and help improve support infrastructures such as information technology and administrative processes.

QUALITY SERVICE IMPROVEMENT

The previous work of the NHS Institute together with the expertise that can be accessed from the IHI provided the health service with a great number of tools and methodologies to begin to address recent failings and make improvements. There needs to be considerable investment in service improvement, and seeing quality improvement as the solution to reducing costs needs to be a view held across the whole of the NHS leadership. Mainstreaming service quality improvements is often the challenge for busy hospitals focusing on 'today', and balancing operational pressures against the need for an embedded longer term quality strategy needs to be the priority. Berwick (2012) believes the responsibility of healthcare leaders to be to establish the context for both the workforce and the public. They need to shape the culture and embed organisational ethics into their organisations. He describes a number of areas that need to be urgently tackled, including the current problems of overtreatment of patients, leading to subjecting patients to unnecessary, inconvenient and uncomfortable diagnostic tests which are adding huge costs to the healthcare budget. Berwick also highlights the high cost of failing to coordinate care, leading to fragmentation, duplication and frequently patients becoming lost in the system. He also believes that failures in care delivery need to be addressed effectively by health professionals, who have a huge role to play in this. Berwick adds the need to reduce administration costs (e.g. reduce endless 'form filling'), address excessive healthcare prices and the urgent need to tackle fraud and abuse of resources. Berwick believes every organisation should have a strategy that incorporates these areas which engage clinicians in what he calls 'the ethics of improvement'. Berwick cites examples of where in the United States medical colleges have led the way in tackling the overdiagnosis of disease and gives examples of some of the early achievements so far.

The key to the success of IHI is the very visible engagement of senior clinicians who are leading many of the safety, culture and service improvement initiatives. If there is a will to really tackle the culture of the NHS, there needs to be a similar strategy that mainstreams quality service improvement in the UK healthcare systems.

GOVERNMENT

The government needs to ensure far greater inclusion of senior clinical professionals, doctors, nurses and others at senior policy-making level, and their advice needs to be clearly documented and open to scrutiny. Similar to many of the previous reports into health service failings, the Francis report demonstrates the many confusing levels of accountabilities that exist. Helpfully Francis has not sought to find a specific scapegoat or 'someone to blame' in response to these failings, and instead has fully adopted the concept of the 'learning organisation'. This approach is helpful in keeping the focus on moving forward with the priority being to ensure that this type of failing is never allowed to happen again. Determining the difference between blame and accountability is important, and it is vital to gain knowledge from errors to prevent future failings. This can seem difficult for those whose relatives have been seriously harmed in these situations, but the important difference relates to the concept of 'intent to do harm' and negligence. While some of the nurses and doctors involved in these failings have been referred for disciplinary and code of conduct hearings, the Francis report highlights a wide range of stakeholders who held accountability for assuring this organisation and yet these failed in nearly every case.

The Francis report (2013) highlighted that many health organisations focused their attention on achieving targets and financial balance at the expense of assuring safe, quality care for their patients. This was part of a whole range of unintended consequences in introducing financial and performance targets from the centre of government and directing health authorities to ensure they were implemented. It is inconceivable that any-one would have anticipated that the pressure to meet financial balance and achieve these targets would have resulted in such serious failings in care delivery. The most important learning to be gained is that govern-ment policy needs to be subjected to far more intense scrutiny and risk assessment and include safeguards, checks and balances and perhaps most importantly be regularly reviewed. No one would advocate return-ing to the times of patients on trolleys in A&E for days, or over 18-month waiting lists for elective operations, but it needs to be recognised that every target may include a set of unintended consequences. One example of this is the target regarding 'mixed sex accommodation' in the pursuit of improving privacy and dignity for patients. An unintended consequence of this is patients being placed on wards that do not have particular spe-ciality skills needed for a particular condition (e.g. cardiology), and busy doctors having to undertake 'safari type' ward rounds trying to locate their patients across a large site. The patient may have been far better served by being placed on the cardiology ward, but was unable to as there was no female bed. The risk of not receiving safe, quality care may be far higher than that of the reduced dignity of sharing a ward with patients of the opposite sex. The point is that further debate is needed, and patients needs to be involved in making the right choices for them-selves. Subjecting government policy to this level of scrutiny is essential and there needs to be a formal mechanism for involving, listening to and engaging the professions that will be expected to deliver these targets.

The government needs to take urgent action in relation to minimum nursing staffing levels. While there may be economic constraints, the evidence regarding the longer term savings, in achieving improvements in mortality and morbidity and reduction of harm, provides a very powerful argument. At IHI Auckland Berwick (2012) stated the need to meet the real challenge of addressing escalating healthcare costs against a backdrop of economic crisis. In his keynote speech he spoke of the need for a social movement to drive the 'ethics of improvement' that includes addressing a number of what he calls 'theoretical water canyons' leading to excessive waste in the healthcare system. Berwick believes that waste is 'theft' and that there is an urgent need to mobilise in particular the clinical leaders in beginning to tackle this huge issue. The amount of money that could be saved if these areas were addressed is enormous, and would help to ensure that the taxpayers' money is spent wisely.

For leaders of healthcare simply implementing yet another set of recommendations is not going to be enough to prevent the failings that continue to be repeated. A wholesale culture change is needed, and this requires the absolute best leadership to see it through. This book is aimed at all leaders in healthcare at every level. The number of healthcare scandals has given a mandate for all leaders to radically change the way the health service is led at every level. No longer can hospitals be dominated by top down finance and performance targets at the expense of safe, quality care. No longer can nurses and doctors tolerate poor standards of care without formally raising their concerns and ensuring action is taken.

Conclusion

The aim of this book was to explore and understand the context in order to help diagnose some of the problems with leadership which have led to healthcare failings. The purpose has been to seek some evidence that will help prescribe a more effective approach for the NHS leadership of today. This book has particularly focused on the area of influence and impact that 'top team' executive leaders can have on the culture of an organisation and consequently the delivery of safe and high-quality care at the front line. However, the principles apply to all leaders no matter where they are in the system, as all have the capacity to make a difference.

The health service needs the right leadership at every level, and the characteristics, values and behaviours of top leaders are critical in directly influencing high-quality frontline care.

The potential adverse effects of dysfunctional leadership are hugely costly in terms of causing serious harm and letting down the patients we seek to serve. It is critical that the NHS not only selects and appoints the right people for leadership but also continually monitors their impact on the frontline delivery of care.

In particular the professions of medicine and nursing care need to recognise fully what has gone wrong, and what needs to be done to make sure failings of this scale can never happen again. Both professions need to be more ambitious, strive for excellence and make sure their clinical knowledge, expertise and experience inform health policy and service delivery effectively at every level. Looking the other way is not an option and professionals need to be held accountable for not only the care they deliver but also for the actions they observe in others. They have a duty to speak up and all leaders in healthcare have a duty to listen and take action when there are any suggestions that care falls below acceptable standards.

Leaders at all levels need to understand fully the features and characteristics of effective leadership and the values they need to hold and demonstrate. They must also understand and articulate the difference between blame and accountability in their organisations, departments and clinical areas.

To achieve this we need to attract and recruit leaders with the best potential, who demonstrate the features and characteristics that engage organisations and align them to the core purpose of delivering the absolute best quality healthcare. These leaders will have humility and a high degree of self-awareness that all leaders are 'incomplete' and it is only in recognising the importance of the collective strengths of teams that the culture of the NHS can hope to make the changes needed.

The appendices in this book include tools for all to use to help them in both the selection and monitoring of leadership teams. The selection tool is equally applicable for any leadership positions and can be adapted for a variety of leadership posts.

Excellence in healthcare team leadership

LEADERSHIP INTERVIEW QUESTIONS

1. What do you believe to be your top three leadership qualities which have led you to your current or most senior top leadership position?
2. What do you believe to be the key features in the leadership of top performing health organisations in terms of their leadership and impact on frontline care delivery?
3. Can you give any examples?
4. What do you think are the key leadership features of poorly performing organisations in terms of impact on the frontline care delivery?
5. Can you give any examples?
6. What do you believe are the ideal characteristics for a top leadership team; for example, a hospital executive team, chief executive, medical or nursing director?
7. What do you think is the percentage of health organisations that have highly effective top team leadership?
8. Why do you think that some leaders fail to impact on making improvements to direct care delivery?
9. What do you believe could be done to improve both the selection and

ongoing monitoring of top leadership teams in relation specifically to their impact on quality and safety delivery to the front line?

10. When appointing to top leadership positions what qualities within the individual would you look for?

11. In addition to current selection processes, such as the standard psychometric testing, 360 degree feedback, and interview, what further processes could be used to assess specific leadership qualities?

12. What approach would you propose for ongoing monitoring of top team leadership effectiveness?

13. How useful would you find a framework/tool based on assessing leadership characteristics in terms of :
    - selection of top leaders
    - ongoing monitoring of leadership effectiveness?

Thank you for taking the time to complete this.

Could you please attach a brief biography?

Selection for leadership roles in healthcare organisations: tool kit/framework

DETERMINING ROLE/POST REQUIRED

1. Undertake a detailed analysis of the current team and full analysis (recognising theories on stages of decline, and incomplete leaders) and identify deficits where weaknesses in the team are identified.
2. Agree with the leadership team the core purpose, such as safety, quality and values, and clearly articulate those which reflect the behaviours expected in the organisation.
3. Develop a detailed job description, with explicit description of areas of leadership, values and engagement.
4. Ensure clarity of expectation is explicit in the job advertisement, which makes the values and behaviour required prominent.

SELECTION PROCESS

- Job description, detailing requirements based on characteristics of successful leaders.
- Detailed scrutiny of CV, checking evidence of track record and

qualifications, and verifying evidence with employers from the previous 5 years.

- Evidence of 360 degree feedback including frontline staff from current post (recognising limitations).
- Objective independent testing of evidence, values, integrity, vision, self-awareness, learning, intellectual/political capacity, ability to cope with change, make difficult decisions, courage, willingness to receive challenge, and personal exposure to challenges.
- Testing of leadership levels (i.e. do not appoint level 1 or level 2 leaders of Maxwell's (2011) framework.
- Observation/cases study of applicant in current work setting.
- Scrutiny of evidence of organisational achievements.

INTERVIEW

Interview techniques include :

- listening
- critical evaluation, being alert for charm
- asking candidate at day of interview for a three- to four-page statement to include:
  1. achievements
  2. why they want job
  3. a description of their work ethic.

Assess leadership level (1–5) (Maxwell, 2011).

SPECIFICALLY TEST FOR THE FOLLOWING

- Ethical values – what does it mean to do the right thing for the right reason?
- Relational values – how do you build an environment of trust and respect for others?

- Success values – what goals are worth spending your life on?

REFERENCES

Include some specific tailored reference questions for the applicant's previous workplace, including the following (Clarke 2005).

- Does x take responsibility for their behaviour?
- Does x ever play one person off against another?
- Has x ever taken credit for others' work?
- Has x ever been subject to performance review?
- Is x prepared to do whatever it takes?
- Would you describe x as a good talker?
- Does x act without thinking about the consequences of their behaviour?
- Have you ever felt intimidated by x?
- Does x ever lose their temper for short periods of time to make people afraid of them?

Monitoring of leadership teams: systematic assessment of culture regarding the organisation, safety and quality

EXAMINE EVIDENCE

1. Definition and agreed standard for values, behaviour and organisational purpose/identity (i.e. clarity of what the organisation stands for)
2. Successful auditing of the three standards above
3. Speak directly to frontline staff, asking what they believe to be good about the trust and what needs to be improved
4. Speak directly to patients and carers, asking what they believe to be good about the trust and what needs to be improved
5. 360 degree feedback leadership teams
6. Royal College reports
7. Student nurse/junior doctors feedback regarding clinical placements
8. Patient forum feedback
9. Table top exercise – safety and quality measures
10. Clinical site visits.

Test for signs of weak corporate culture (Hopkins, Hopkins and Mallette, 2005):

- no clear value or beliefs, or
- so many beliefs but lack of agreement
- subcultures with different beliefs
- subcultures pull in different directions (managers need intercultural competence)
- behaviour from senior leaders that is inconsistent with the vision of the organisation.

Test alignment with workers:

- values (what is important)
- identity (what organisation stands for)
- behaviour (what is okay and not okay)
- peer review
- detecting control and command/level 1 leadership.

Summary of recommendations

- Review of roles of chairs and non-executives to include time allocated, training, and development.
- Review of roles of board secretary and consistent approach across trusts.
- Executive teams to undertake an honest appraisal and diagnosis of the strengths and weaknesses of their members.
- A bespoke development programme needs to be an integral part of the NHS Leadership Academy which includes chairs, non-executives and board secretaries.
- Develop and improve the current appraisal system for chairs and non-executives supported by the academy.
- Secondment of the most effective chief executives into challenged trusts needs to be considered.
- Leadership development at all levels of organisations.
- Specific training for all panel members on selection/interview techniques.
- Monitoring of boards and organisational culture.
- Formal appraisal system, and proper mentorship and supervision for executives.
- A formal mentoring programme needs to be set up for new chief executives (and teams), pairing them with the most successful and experienced.

- A review of how boards could be better structured and balanced to support safety and quality.
- Nationally agreed set of data and quality indicators agreed (with some room for local ownership) with the CCG, which includes reports from the wide range of external stakeholders.
- Greater analysis and use by the trusts of their own data, interpreted for their own board assurance.
- Boards should use 'run charts' to track progress/deterioration of performance, rather than red, amber, green (RAG) ratings.
- Board should use reports from external stakeholders, such as royal colleges, to check culture.
- NHS staff surveys to include additional question on action taken after respondents have stated they wouldn't wish their relative to be cared for in their hospital.
- Greater representation of nursing at all levels and in particular at government level.
- The government to ensure they have in place senior nursing leadership and advice at policy level.
- A review of the international learning about nursing, as other countries (e.g. United States and Australia) have addressed similar problems.
- Introduction of legislation for minimum registered nursing and midwifery staffing levels.
- Expansion of programmes such as offered with the Florence Nightingale scholarships.
- Comprehensive impact evaluation of the range of previous initiatives which have been implemented, such as LEO.
- Introduction of planned formal clinical sessions as part of the role in a similar way to that of the medical director. (This should also include senior nurses in commissioning roles.)
- Pairing of non-executive with directors and allocating a group of wards to them to give opportunities for direct feedback to the board from patients.
- Revalidation for nursing to be funded at same per head cost as medicine.

- Re-energising of nursing research to promote evidence-based practice in clinical care and leadership and in organisational learning.
- Review the role and time allocated for medical director in trusts.
- Medical directors' job roles need to include accountability for mortality and morbidity of patients, effective job planning and implementing 7-day consultant working, ensuring consultants take full accountability for the patients in their care.
- More attention needs to be given to the development of consultants for these roles; while they are usually highly skilled consultants many find that they are relatively inexperienced in the reality of working at executive level.
- Engaging the clinical workforce.
- There is a need to develop a specific strategy to actively engage lead clinicians using the six-phase framework.
- Leadership development needs to be undertaken at all levels, and actively engaging junior doctors is very important. Often these doctors have the benefit of 'fresh eyes' and by working in a number of trusts they are able to very quickly assess where improvements can be made. As such they need a forum.
- A productive medicine module based on the nursing ones (similar to that designed by the former NHS Institute) needs to be developed and introduced.
- Government policy needs to be subjected to far more intense scrutiny and risk assessment and include safeguards, checks and balances and perhaps most importantly be reviewed regularly.
- The government needs to lead a social movement to drive the 'ethics of improvement' and reduce waste in the health service.

References and further reading

Aiken S (2012) *Nursing in metamorphosis: the profession and its image explored.* Doctoral thesis, University of Brighton.

Alimo-Metcalfe B (2012) *Engaging boards: the relationship between governance and leadership and improving the quality and safety of patient care.* Supporting Paper for the King's Fund Leadership Review. London: King's Fund.

Alvesson M (1993) *Cultural perspectives on organisations.* Cambridge: Cambridge University Press.

Ancona D, Malone T, Orlikowski J, Senge P (2007) In praise of the incomplete leader. *Harv Bus Rev.* **85**(2): 92–100.

Argyris C (1957) *Personality and organization.* New York: HarperCollins.

Bagraim J (2001) Organisational psychology and workplace control: the instrumentality of corporate culture. *S Afr J Psychol.* **31**(3): 43–9.

Bass BM (1990) From transactional to transformational leadership: learning to share the vision. *Organ Dyn.* **18**(3): 19–36.

Bass BM, Avolio BJ (1993) Transformational leadership and organisational culture. *Public Admin Quart.* **17**(1): 112–21.

Bennett N, Wise C, Wood P, Harvey J (2003) *Distributed leadership: full report.* Nottingham: National College for School Leadership.

Bennis WG (1961) Revisionist theory of leadership. *Harv Bus Rev.* **39**: 26–36, 146–50.

Bennis WG, Nanus B (1985) *Leaders: the strategies for taking charge.* New York: Harper & Row.

Berry T, Bunning R *Leadership.* Edinburgh Business School. Available at: www. ebsglobal.net/EBS/media/EBS/PDFs/Leadership-Course-Taster.pdf

Berwick D (2012) Keynote speaker: The APAC Forum on Quality Improvement in Health Care. 19–21 September 2012, Auckland, New Zealand.

Bisognano M (2012) Keynote speaker: The APAC Forum on Quality Improvement in Health Care. 19–21 September 2012, Auckland, New Zealand.

Bohmer R (2012) *The instrumental value of medical leadership: engaging doctors in improving services.* London: The King's Fund. Available at: www.kingsfund.org.uk/sites/files/kf/instrumental-value-medical-leadership-richard-bohmer-leadership-review2012-paper.pdf

Bolden R, Wood M, Gosling J (2006) Is the NHS Leadership Qualities Framework missing the wood for the trees? In: Casebeer A, Harrison A, Mark AL. *Innovations in health care: a reality check.* New York: Palgrave Macmillan. pp. 17–29.

Bosch M, Dijkstra R, Wensing M, Van der Weijden T, Grol R (2008) Organizational culture, team climate and diabetes care in small office-based practices. *BMC Health Serv Res.* **8**: 180. doi: 10.1186/1472-6963-8-180. Available at: www.biomedcentral.com/1472-6963/8/180

Brenner R (2005) *The blaming organizational coping pattern.* Cambridge, MA: Chaco Canyon Consulting. Available at: www.chacocanyon.com/essays/orgblaming.shtml

Caldwell G (2006) Real-time assessment and feedback of junior doctors improves clinical performance. *Clin Teacher.* **3**(3): 185–8.

Cameron K, Quinn R (1999) *Diagnosing and changing organisational cultures: based on the competing values framework.* Reading, MA: Wiley.

Carter P (2011) Newly trained nurses 'not up to the mark'. *Student Nursing Times,* 22 September. Press Association.

Chaffer D (2012) Reflections. Advanced solutions: patients' increasingly complex care needs mean nurses must be well educated. *Nursing Standard.* **26**(24).

Clark J (2012) *Medical engagement: too important to be left to chance.* London: The King's Fund. Available at: www.kingsfund.org.uk/sites/files/kf/medical-engagement-nhs-john-clark-leadership-review2012-paper.pdf

Clarke J (2005) *Working with monsters.* Sydney: Random House Australia.

Collins J (2000) Built to flip. *Fast Company.* March. Available at: www.fastcompany.com/38659/built-flip

Collins J (2001) *Good to great: why some companies make the leap . . . and other don't.* New York: HarperCollins.

Collins J, Hansen MT (2011) *Great by choice: uncertainty, chaos, and luck – why some thrive despite them all.* New York: HarperCollins.

Commission for Health Care Improvement (2002) *Gosport War Memorial Investigation into the Health Care NHS Trust.* London: Stationery Office Books.

Davies HTO, Mannion R, Jacobs R, Powell AE, Marshall MN (2007) Exploring the relationship between senior management team culture and hospital performance. *Med Care Res Rev.* **64**(1): 46–65.

Dekker S (2007) *Just culture: balancing safety and accountability*. Aldershot: Ashgate.

Department of Health (DoH) (2000) *An organisation with a memory: report of an expert group on learning from adverse events in the NHS*. London: The Stationery Office.

Department of Health (DoH) (2012) *Transforming care: a national response to Winterbourne View Hospital. Department of Health Review Final Report*. London: Department of Health. Available at: www.gov.uk/government/uploads/system/uploads/attachment_data/file/213215/final-report.pdf

Department of Health (DoH) (2015) *Making healthcare more human-centred and not system-centred*. Speech. Department of Health and the Rt Hon Jeremy Hunt MP at King's Fund. London: Department of Health. Available at: www.gov.uk/government/speeches/making-healthcare-more-human-centred-and-not-system-centred

Drucker P (2003) *Peter Drucker on the profession of management*. Cambridge, MA: Harvard Business Review Press.

Dyer WG Jr., Wilkins AL (1991) Better stories, not better constructs, to generate better theory: a rejoinder to Eisenhardt. *Acad Manage Rev.* **16**(3): 613–19.

Edwards JN, Silow-Caroll S, Lashbrook A (2011) *Achieving efficiency: lessons from four top-performing hospitals. Synthesis Report*. Boston: The Commonwealth Fund.

Fenton K (2007) *Patient care portfolio: AUKUH Acuity/Dependency Tool implementation resource pack*. London: The Association of UK University Hospitals. Available at: www.aukuh.org.uk/index.php/directors-of-nursing/42-implementation-resource-pack

Francis R (2010) *Independent Inquiry into Care Provided by Mid Staffordshire NHS Foundation Trust January 2005 to March 2009*. Vol. I and II. London: The Stationery Office.

Francis R (2013) *Report of the Mid Staffordshire NHS Foundation Trust Public Inquiry*. Vol. 1–III and Executive Summary. Available at: www.gov.uk/government/publications/report-of-the-mid-staffordshire-nhs-foundation-trust-public-inquiry

Frankel AS, Leonard MW, Denham CR (2006) Fair and just culture, team behavior, and leadership engagement: the tools to achieve high reliability. *Health Serv Res.* **41**(4 Pt 2): 1690–1709. Available at: www.ncbi.nlm.nih.gov/pmc/articles/PMC1955339/

Glaser J (2006) *The DNA of leadership: leverage your instincts to communicate, differentiate, innovate*. Avon, MA: Platinum Press.

Griffiths R (2011) *NHS Management Inquiry*. London: HMSO.

Gronn P (2008) The future of distributed leadership. *J Educ Admin.* **46**(2): 141–58.

Guardian (2012) Eleven NHS foundation trusts have serious financial problems, MPs told. 18 September. Available at: www.guardian.co.uk/society/2012/sep/18/nhs-foundation-trusts-financial-problems

Hampden-Turner C (1990) *Creating corporate culture.* Reading, MA: Addison-Wesley.

Harrison R (1972) Understanding your organization's character. *Harv Bus Rev.* **5**(3): 119–28.

Hopkins W, Hopkins S, Mallette P (2005) *Aligning organizational subcultures for competitive advantage: a strategic change approach.* New York: Basic Books.

House R (1995) Leadership in the 21st century. A speculative enquiry. In: Howard A, editor. *The changing nature of work.* San Francisco: Jossey-Bass.

Howard LW (1998) Validating the competing values model as a representation of organizational cultures. *Int J Org Analys.* **6**(3): 231–50.

Institute of Management & Administration (IMA) (2002) How a values-based culture pays off. *HR Focus.* **79**(10): 1–5.

Kahneman D (2011) *Thinking, fast and slow.* New York: Farrar, Straus and Giroux.

Kean S, Haycock SE (2011) Understanding the relationship between followers and leaders. *Nurs Manag.* **18**(8): 31–5.

Kennedy I (chair) (2001) *The Report of the Public Inquiry into Children's Heart Surgery at the Bristol Royal Infirmary 1984–1995. Learning from Bristol.* London: The Stationery Office. Available at: http://webarchive.nationalarchives.gov.uk/+/www.dh.gov.uk/en/Publicationsandstatistics/Publications/PublicationsPolicyAndGuidance/DH_4005620

Kim K, Danseruau F, Kim IS, Kim KS (2004) A multiple-level theory of leadership: the impact of culture as a moderator. *J Leadership Organ Stud.* **11**(1): 78–93.

King's Fund (2011) *The future of leadership and management in the NHS: no more heroes.* London: The King's Fund.

Laming, Lord (2003) The Victoria Climbie inquiry: report of an inquiry by Lord Laming. DoH Crown Publication. Available at: www.gov.uk/government/publications/the-victoria-climbie-inquiry-report-of-an-inquiry-by-lord-laming

Leape LL (2009) Errors in medicine. *Clinica Chimica Acta.* **404**(1): 2–5.

Legge K (1995) *Human resource management: the rhetorics, the realities.* 2nd ed. London: Macmillan.

Leversidge A (2012) Midwives and disciplinary proceedings. *Midwives Magazine.* **6**, 8 Nov.

Liker JK (2004) *The Toyota Way: 14 management principles from the world's greatest manufacturer.* New York: McGraw-Hill.

MacBeath J (2005) Leadership as distributed: a matter of practice. *Sch Leader Manag.* **25**(4): 349–66.

McMurry RN (1958) The case for benevolent autocracy. *Harv Bus Rev.* **36**(1): 82–90.

Marx D (2009) Whack-a-mole: the price we pay for expecting perfection. Available at: www.whackamolethebook.com/

Maxwell JC (2011) *The 5 Levels of Leadership: proven steps to maximise your potential.* New York: Center Street.

Maynard R (2005) *Life at the top: triumphs, travails and teachings of Australia's business leaders.* Sydney: New Holland Publishers Australia.

National Audit Office (2003) The management of suspensions of clinical staff in NHS hospital and ambulance trusts in England: report by the Controller and Auditor General. Available at: www.nao.org.uk/wp-content/uploads/2003/11/02031143.pdf

National Patient Safety Agency (NPSA) (2004) *Seven steps to patient safety: a guide for NHS staff.* NPSA. Available at: www.nrls.npsa.nhs.uk/EasySiteWeb/GatewayLink.aspx?alId=59970

National Patient Safety Agency (NPSA) (2008) *Foresight training: resource pack.* Available at: www.nrls.npsa.nhs.uk/EasySiteWeb/getresource.axd?AssetID=60160

NHS Institute (2006) *NHS Institute for Innovation and Improvement (2006–2013) productive ward series: releasing time to care.* NHS Institute.

Ogbonna E, Wilkinson B (2003) The false promise of organizational culture change: a case study of middle managers in grocery retailing. *J Manage Stud.* **40**(5): 1151–78.

Organ DW (1994) Organizational citizenship behavior and the good soldier. In: Rumsey MG, Walker CB, Harris J, editors. *Personnel selection and classification.* Hillsdale, NJ: Lawrence Erlbaum Associates, Inc. pp. 53–67.

Owen D (2008) *In sickness and in power: illnesses in heads of government during the last 100 years.* London: Methuen.

Parry KW, Proctor-Thomson SB (2003) Leadership, culture and performance: the case of the New Zealand public sector. *J Change Manage.* **3**(4): 376–99.

Pascale RT (1985) Paradox of corporate culture. reconciling ourselves to socialization. *Calif Manage Rev.* **27**: 38–64.

Pech R, Slade BW (2007) Organisational sociopaths: rarely challenged, often promoted. Why? *Soc Bus Rev.* **2**(3): 254–69.

Peters T, Waterman R (1982) *In search of excellence.* New York: Harper & Row.

Pettigrew A (1997) What is processual analysis? *Scand J Manage.* **13**(4): 337–48.

Rayner C (2008) *Stop your gossiping, nurse! But that's just one symptom of the bigger*

crisis facing the NHS. Available at: www.dailymail.co.uk/health/article-1016278/
CLAIRE-RAYNER-Stop-gossiping-nurse-But-thats-just-symptom-bigger-crisis-
facing-NHS.html#ixzz3vu8JT64y

Reason J (1997) *Managing the risks of organizational accidents.* Aldershot: Ashgate.

Reinertsen JL, Gosfield AG, Rupp W, Whittington JW (2007) *Engaging physicians
in a shared quality agenda. IHI Innovation Series White Paper.* Cambridge. MA:
Institute for Healthcare Improvement.

Robb E (2013) Act on the evidence and introduce minimum nurse staffing levels.
Nursing Times. 29 January.

Robbins SP (1996) *Organizational behaviour concepts, controversies and applications.*
7th ed. Englewood Cliffs, NJ: Prentice Hall.

Royal College of Nursing (RCN) (2012) *Care Campaign Survey results.* http://journals.
rcni.com/page/ns/campaigns/care-campaign/features/survey-results

Royal College of Physicians (RCP) (2012) *Hospitals on the edge? The time for action.
A report by the Royal College of Physicians.* London: RCP.

Santry C (2007) Clinicians should be groomed for top jobs says Nicholson. *Health
Service J.* 1 Jan. Available at: www.hsj.co.uk/news/clinicians-should-be-groomed-
for-top-jobs-says-nicholson/57488.article

Schein EH (1993) On dialogue, culture and organizational learning. *Organ Dyn.*
22(2): 40–51.

Scott T, Mannion R, Davies H, Marshall M (2003) The quantitative measurement
of organizational culture in health care: a review of available instruments. *Health
Serv Res.* **38**(3): 923–45.

Senge P (1990) *The fifth discipline: the art and practice of the learning organization.*
1st ed. Doubleday/Currency: New York.

Silvester J, Anderson N, Patterson F (1999) Organizational culture change: an inter-
group attributional analysis. *J Occup Organ Psychol.* **72**(1): 1–24.

Spetz J, Chapman S, Herrara C, Kaiser J, Seago J, Dower C (2009) *Assessing the
impact of California's nursing staff ratios on hospitals and patient care.* Oakland:
California HealthCare Foundation.

Spillane JP (2006) *Distributed leadership.* San Francisco: Jossey-Bass.

Taitz J, Lee T, Sequist T (2001) A framework for engaging physicians in quality and
safety. *BMH Quality & Safety.* 1: 722–8. Available at: http://qualitysafety.bmj.com/
content/early/2011/07/13/bmjqs-2011-000167

Timmins N (2012) *Never again? The story of the Health and Social Care Act 2012.*
London: The King's Fund.

Tomlinson G (2012) *A book report on How the Mighty Fall (and why some companies never give in) by Jim Collins.* Available at: https://docs.google.com/file/d/0BwIMF crVfsnDb3lPclp5SHNlU0E/edit?pli=1

Twigg D, Duffield C, Bremner A, Rapley P, Finn J (2011) The impact of the nursing hours per patient day (NHPPD) staffing methods on patient outcomes: a retrospective analysis of patient and staff data. *Int J Nurs Stud.* **48**(5): 540–8. doi: 10.1016/j.ijnurstu.2010.07.013.

Valle M (1999) Crisis, culture and charisma: the new leader's work in public organizations. *Public Pers Manage.* **28**(2): 245–57.

Van Wart M (2003) Public-sector leadership theory: an assessment. *Publ Admin Rev.* **63**(2): 214–28.

Wachter RM, Pronuvust P (2009) Balancing 'no blame' with accountability in patient safety. *New Engl J Med.* **361**: 1401–6.

Whitlock J (2013) The value of active followership. *Nurs Manag.* **20**(2): 17–28.

Willcocks SG (2012) Exploring leadership effectiveness: nurses as clinical leaders in the NHS. *Leadership in Health Services.* **25**(1): 8–19.

Willis Commission (2012) *Quality with compassion: the future of nursing education. Report of the Willis Commission.* Available at: www.williscommission.org. uk/recommendations

Yankelovich D (1991) *Coming to public judgment: making democracy work in a complex world.* Syracuse, NY: Syracuse University Press.

Young H (2009) (Un) Critical Times? Situated Distributed Leadership in the field. *Journal of Educational Administration and History.* **41**: 377–89.

Zammuto RF, Krakower JY (1991) Quantitative and qualitative studies of organizational culture. In: Woodman RW, Pasmore WA, editors. *Research in organizational change and development.* Vol. 5. Greenwich, CT: JAI Press.

Index